AND

Advance Praise for *And*

The philosophy and magic of improvisation relies on the cardinal principle of *Yes, and*. TZiPi Radonsky's new work, *And*, explores the power of the terrain of *Yes* in everyday life. Part memoir, part self-help, part spiritual journey, *And* provides wisdom from a unique voice.

— Patricia Ryan Madson, Stanford Emerita and author of *Improv Wisdom: Don't Prepare, Just Show Up*

These poetic reflections are like fine chocolate — bite-sized, delicate, and intense. The ingredients are the product of a life of action and reflection, pain and joy, growth and ever-deepening wisdom. They are best sampled as TZiPi created them, as treats to be savored slowly, in small bites, their effects lingering in mind and memory long after they've been consumed. I hope you enjoy them as much as I did.

— Lyndon Rego, global director, Leadership Beyond Boundaries, Center for Creative Leadership

Jacob Frank, the great Jewish heretic, once wrote that one must "hold on to this and not remove one's hand from that." In that spirit of inclusion and productive transgression comes this fascinating book's embrace of the *vav*, the *and*, the nondual. Enjoy and be challenged.

— Jay Michaelson, author of *Everything is God: The Radical Path of Nondual Judaism*

And isn't a book about Jewish mysticism, it is a Jewish mystical book. Reading *And* takes you into the soul of a contemporary kabbalist. You feel what it is to engage the world with a mystic heart. Rabbi Radonsky has opened a window into the mystical the way few others can or will. Read this book, and be grateful that you did.

— Rabbi Rami Shapiro, author of *Amazing Chesed*

Rabbi TZiPi Radonsky describes herself as a lifelong learner, and in this rare collection of intense musings over a five-year period, she digs unblinkingly into her own heart and mind, raising fundamental questions about spirituality, how we live our lives, our independence and connectedness, and much more. Driving the work is *vav*, the Hebrew word for *and*, the great connector. Throughout these writings, one can see the power of *vav* in her life and, through her blessings, in ours. Expanding our hearts to include all others; expanding our minds to be open to all possibilities.

— Barry Oshry, author of
Seeing Systems: Unlocking the Mysteries of Organizational Life

The book *And* is a joy. No *buts* about it! This is real life being lived, with delicious breadcrumbs for us all to follow. The wisdom it contains is profound, accessible, and honest. Open your heart!

And is a book of revelation, and a guidebook for any spiritual traveler. From the wellspring of the Torah, *And* flows to all hearts. Bursting with song, for all the lonely people, halleluya: It is going to be alright. This book is a joy!

And is a profound and joyful book that brings together spirit and leadership, examining the path that joins greatness, humility, and compassion. *And* asks important questions, then sits with us as the answers gently come forth. How do you protect your heart? How do you open your heart? *And* will engage you right there, in the heart.

— Chuck Palus, senior faculty and manager of the Connected Leadership Project at the Center for Creative Leadership and co-author of
Making Common Sense: Leadership as Meaning-making in a Community of Practice and
The Leader's Edge: Six Creative Competencies for Exploring Complex Challenges

The title *And*, the rich Hebrew wisdom running through the book, and the inspiring imagery of this five-year journal drew me quickly into the author's own spiritual quest for an inclusive heart. Through stories, poetry, and inspiring illustrations at the beginning of each chapter, Rabbi TZiPi Radonsky continually and reflectively invites the reader into a deep awareness of the power of the inclusive word *and*. Her constant monitoring of her own vocabulary and personal attitude reminds us of our need also to recognize and transform our own human limits and personal boxes. Using the Hebrew letter *vav* and a prayerful meditation at the end of many chapters also challenges us to find a blessing each day through the inclusive teaching of mystical Jewish wisdom.

— Sister Elizabeth M. Reis, SSJ, D.MIN, director of The S.S.J. Consultant Services and author of *A Deeper Kind of Truth and The Gift of a Listening Heart*

AND

Building a World of Connection through Jewish Mystical Wisdom

Rabbi TziPi Vivien Radonsky, Ph.D.

an Arthur Kurzweil book
New York/Jerusalem

Copyright © 2013 by Rabbi TZiPi Vivien Radonsky, Ph.D.
All rights reserved

AN ARTHUR KURZWEIL BOOK
11 Bond Street #456
Great Neck, NY 11021

First edition

No part of this book may be used or reproduced in any manner whatsoever without the prior express written permission of the author, except in the case of brief quotations embodied in critical articles and reviews. Please do not participate in or encourage piracy of copyrighted material in violation of the author's rights.

rebtzipi.com
facebook.com/societyofthevav
The author encourages readers to contact her at rebtzipi@gmail.com.

Rabbi TZiPi Vivien Radonsky, Ph.D.
And
Building a World of Connection through Jewish Mystical Wisdom

ISBN 978-0-9855658-5-5

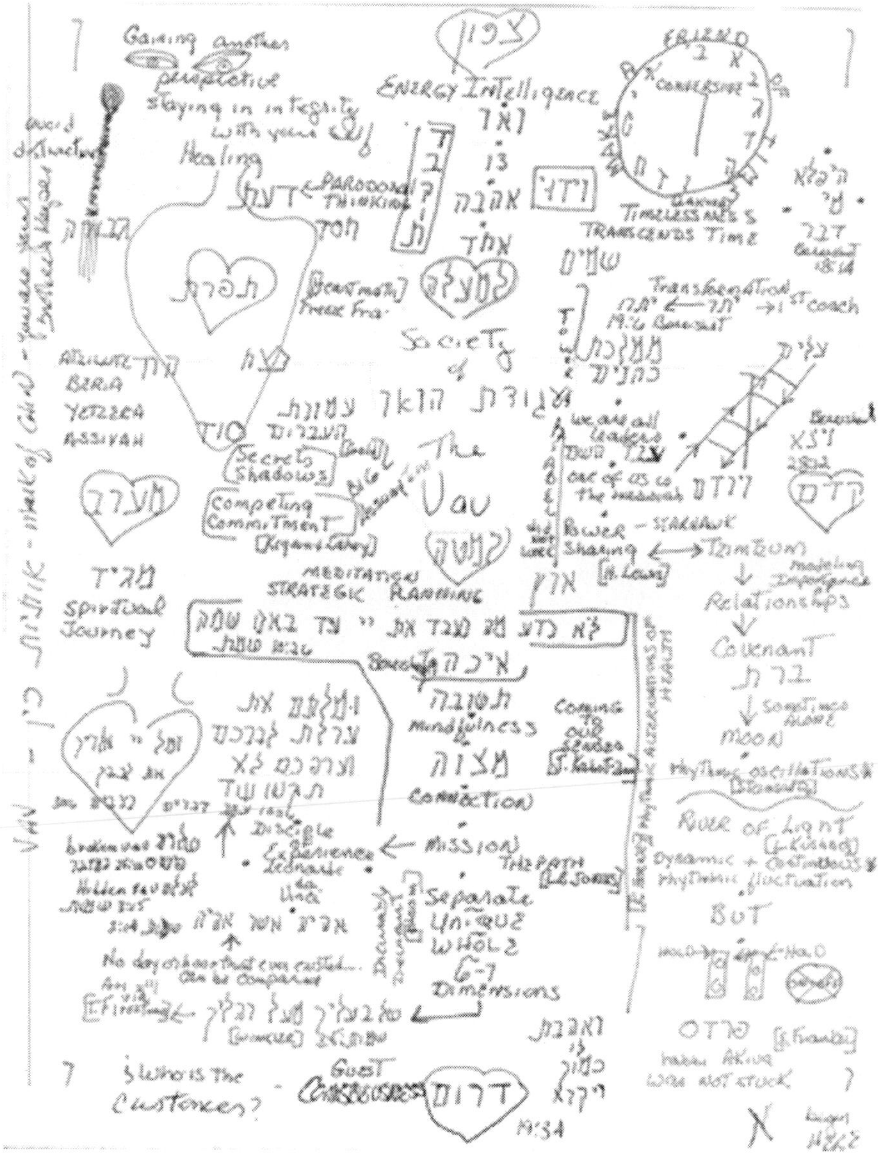
Gaining another perspective
staying in integrity with your
Healing
PARADOXICAL THINKING
צפון
ENERGY INTELLIGENCE
אור
is
אהבה
אחד
FRIEND
TIMELESSNESS
TRANSCENDS TIME
TRANSFORMATION
1ST COACH
Society of
The Vau
Secrets Shadows
Competing Commitment
BERIA
YETZIRA
ASSIYAH
we are all leaders
POWER - STARHAWK
Power Sharing
TZIMTZUM
Relationships
Covenant
ברית
MOON
RIVER OF LIGHT
BUT
Spiritual Journey
MEDITATION
STRATEGIC PLANNING
mindfulness
COMING TO OUR SENSES
CONNECTION
MISSION
THE PATH
Separate
Unique
WHOLE
Dimensions
Who is the Customer?
GUEST
דרום
פרדס
Rabbi Akiva was not stuck

Table of Contents

Acknowledgments xiii

Introduction xv

2007
Step One: Listening 3
Step Two: Be Humble 9
Inclusion 11
Love Yourself, She Needs You! 13
Step Three: Setting Intentions 15
Gates of Tears and *Teshuva* 17
Being One, *Devekute* 19
Including Me on the Daily To-Do List 21
So, What Is a *Vav*? 23
Organizational Coaching: Living "We Need Each Other" 25
The Mystery of the Cards 27
Protecting the Heart at Work 31

2008
We Are One 37
Walking the Walk 39
Transformation and Healing 43
Beginner's Mind 45
Flowing into the Wind 47
Blessings on Your Going and Coming 49
Moving onto Holy Ground 53
Circle of Life: Redeeming the Sparks 55
The American Legacy Inclusive® Dictionary Denounces *But* ... 57
Growing the Tree Outside the Fence 61
Blessing the Naked Soul 65
Teach What You Need to Learn 67
Living One Life: Being a Rabbi Who Loves Her Leadership
　　Development Work 71

This Nearly Was Mine 75
The *Vav* as a Symbol of Paradox 77
Coming-Out Is Getting Easier to Do 79
A Core Value: Kindness 83
Find Yourself a Teacher, Friends 85
Addictions 87
An Artist's Prayer 89
I Know Nothing — or at Least I Need to Pretend I Do 93
Intention: To Save a Life 95
Hungry Ghosts and the Grasshopper Story 97
New Moon: An Opportunity for a Renewal Life 99
A Birth Day 101
Being Included Is Like Breath to Me 105
Finding Allies and Building Bridges 109
Learning to Be Held in Elul 113
Shalom: Saying Goodbye and Hello 117
Residuals of a Life Out of Control 119
Prayer to a Compassionate G!D 121
Getting the Word Out 123
Challenges of Holding Multiple Realities 127
Musing on the Moment 131
Meditation Is Saving My Life 135
There Is Nothing Sorry About You 139

2009
Claiming the Liminal Space of Not Knowing 143
I Feel Known and You Can't Get Better than That 147
I Am Reb TZiPi and I Am Here to Recruit You 151
Letting Myself Back into My Heart 153
And Expands My Heart and My Perspective 155
Transparency and Telling the Truth 159
Building on a Legacy While Finding Balance 163
Memories 167
Relationships Take Time 171
Being 173
MULKA — Mothers United for Loving-Kindness & Allies 175

Strategic Planning 177
Living the Future Today 179
The Weekly New and Good 181
Entering the Promise Land 183
Lamed Vavniks 185
Surprises that Nurture the Soul 189
LOL 193
The Gerund 195
Early Morning Musings 197
Movies as an Antidote to Change 199
We Are Never Alone in Seeking Balance 201
Who's Got Your Back? 203

2010
The Competing Commitment 209
If Doing Is Being, What Is Receiving? 213
And Eventually You Become the Matriarch 215
Afflicting the Comfortable 219
The Meeting of Peace and Reconciliation 223
I Am Smart Just by Asking the Questions 227
Choices 229
Going Deeper with the Words 231
Being Distracted 235
And G!D Was in this Place and I, I Did Not Know 237
Endless Exciting Dreams 241
Taking the Crap off the Soul 245
I Need to Sleep with Competition 247
A Retreat in the Moment 251
Intro to the Kaddish: A *Tzedaka* Project 255
Yes, *and* 259
Do You Talk with G!D? 261
And the Child Will Lead Them 263
Inspiration: Seeing the Garden Through the Doorway 265
"Love is All You Need" Is Not Enough for Me Today 267
A New Name, A New Relationship 271
Collecting the Dots of Being "Gotten" 273

Comings and Goings of Eternity: Meeting Again, Still Tasting Delicious ..277
Reminders of the Joy in Being Me 279
National Coming-Out Day: Smiling at Fear 283
Halleluya, Praise the One Without End 287
Getting the Whole Picture 291
Just Be You 295
It's My Job to Be Me 299
Rushing Off to New Things with the Wisdom of the Past 301
The Importance of Being You, Honoring Difference 303

2011

I Think I Am Falling in Love with G!D! 309
I Am Yearning for the Familiar 313
We Need Each Other *And* Together We Can Do Anything — *Yeah, But*......315
I Am Denouncing My Speed Queen Crown 321
Hit and Run 323
Tiiiime is On My Side, Oh, Yes It Is! 325
The One Day that Is Different 329
Collecting Stories on Time 331
What Keeps Me from Being an Effective Leader? 333
Personal Best 335
The Wall Is Down: The Heart Is Receiving in this Moment 337
Standing on the Threshold 339
Disorientation and the Antidote 341
Circumcise Your Heart and Do Not Have Such a Stiff Neck 343
Practicing Surrender 347
Learning to Play on the Offensive Team 349
A Taste of the World to Come 351
Holy Union, *Hieros Gamos* 355
I Had a Dream 357
Closure 361

Bibliography 367

Acknowledgments

A huge lesson for me in the creation of this book was that I am my own teacher. Through writing I experienced my interconnectedness to everything and everyone. I am learning that I am never alone. I live in the midst of interconnected circles of various communities that nurture and sustain me, inspire and love me, teach, challenge, and hold me. Some of those bright circle lights are: Sarah Yehudit Schneider, my Talmud/mystical Judaism teacher, who was available to talk about the *vav* and, through her wisdom and open heart, encouraged me to keep dancing to the needs of the moment. Friend and colleague Chuck Palus, who taught me about the ins and outs of blogging and gave me feedback on my writing. My *and* partner, Lyndon Rego, who engaged with me about *and* through writing and thinking about the use of *and* in the world. Rabbi Eli Havivi, who — when I told him about my love affair with the *vav* — coined the word *Vav-nik* as a spinoff from Lamed Vavniks, who like other avatars, walk the earth mending tears in the universe. Tim, who taught me about trust and self-soothing while supporting my personal growth through helping me see what he saw. Mary Louise, who helped me create *Vav-nik* cards and then send out the first certificates from the Society of the *Vav*. Rabbi Shefa Gold, who role-modeled a way of thinking and created a structure I was able to emulate as I wrote my blog posts. The many along my path who found time to read the blog and were moved to make comments and those who listened as I encouraged them to join my mission to de-*but* the world. My primary virtual mindfulness teachers, the Baal Shem Tov and the Buddha, who modeled how to stay awake, to trust oneself and to do what was right for me. Marc Gafni, the man who ordained me, who believed that my light needed to be a rabbi, who offered his students the phrase *Hebrew wisdom*. I am grateful for his opening this gate.

As in all rhythmic, oscillating circles my friend Arthur Kurzweil came back into my life and was committed to making this project happen; and my editor-in-chief, Wendy Bernstein, who taught me so much about patience and that relationships grow over time. And my daughters, Andrea and Ilana, and sister Phyllis, who are my constant.

I have often met people who gave gratefulness to their God for their creativity. From the first time I heard that phrase, I wanted that relationship, too. Today, I realize I had it all along. In publishing this book, I am honoring that holy partnership.

Introduction

Welcome to this collection of musings, which I wrote at various times of the day and night between 2007 and 2011. Like many others, I learn best by writing, going deep inside, wrestling with the mind and heart, trying to understand a thought, idea, emotion, situation, or combination of happenings. These musings helped me learn how I could be consciously in alignment with two integral parts of my soul's journey — being an executive mentor coach and a rabbi, teacher of Hebrew wisdom.

The mind is very curious and makes connections between thoughts and reality. It has taken me many years to learn that my job is to learn to live with that curious mind, to make peace with her in every moment through paying attention to what I heard, and to make choices based on my core values of lovingkindness and compassion. Several years ago, in an awakened moment, I heard a phrase that stayed with me and kept running around in my head. I was not sure what it meant, yet the phrase *"Society of the Vav"* had been born into my consciousness and I needed to know what my relationship to it was. The words were gifts, I am sure, to keep me awake and resilient. My curiosity pushed me to action. Today I can say that gift came *from* my heart *to* my heart, via my deep faith in the Mystery of Life.

In Israel in the spring of 2007, I said out loud this phrase that I had been harboring. I received very positive and curious responses from the guests gathered at my teacher's Sabbath evening table. The women's curiosity began watering the seeds for me to continue to explore what Society of the *Vav* actually means. And I thought that perhaps by writing this blog, I would gather the other parts of this puzzle and come to understand my relationship to the Society of the *Vav*.

My learning began by noticing I was walking two parallel paths: leadership and mystical wisdom. If I were to have alignment, I needed to shift the trajectory of these paths so they would touch and I would become enlightened.

One path was working with my corporate clients, where I had begun to notice the negative affect the word *but* had on our conversations. The more *buts* my clients used in the conversation, the more confused they sounded and the more limited they were in moving forward. I also noticed my own *yeah, buts* and how they limited me.

The other path involved my love affair with Hebrew wisdom and the *vav*, the sixth letter of the Hebrew alphabet. In biblical Hebrew the *vav* is used as a connector and is frequently translated as *and*. This love affair was fed by my readings from pop culture and leadership literature that supported the concepts developed in *Boundary Spanning Leadership*; *Connected: A Declaration of Interdependence*; and the *yes, and* exercise from Improv literature. This information re-adjusted my two parallel paths and brought them into a woven space. I felt more in alignment and my energy became focused and strong.

Then it was Rosh Hashana, the beginning of a new year in the Jewish calendar and the celebration of the birth of the world. I felt the auspiciousness of starting a project that I hoped would change my life. During a phone call earlier that day with my teacher in Israel, I began to feel the confidence of a lover, obsessed to begin learning through the physical experience of writing. I needed to hear and see and, therefore, validate my own voice.

Teeth clenching, fingers on keyboard, I began to write — "Step One: Listen."

What you will find on the following pages are my improvisational musings. I love to write. Many people think of me as an extrovert. I do get some of my energy from others, and I also love being by myself, digging deep and scratching the inside of a thought, watching the spreading connections between words and ideas. In this book you will read about the core seed that stimulated my thinking about the use of *and*.

At times there is a form and consistency to the blog, other times I got bored, or could not remember how I did the last entry, so I wrote the next entry differently. Each time I wrote to understand an idea, an experience. I started using pictures because the color and imagery added interest and expanded my imagination and use of words. Unless otherwise noted, all of the artwork in the book — drawings, paintings, photographs — were done by me. Hang in there with my consistent inconsistencies! And really, nothing is ever the same, so why bank on it? LOL!!

Throughout the blog I refer to a number of books, movies, poems, and songs that informed my journey. A list of reference material can be found in the bibliography at the back of the book if you would like to do some further reading.

What I have come to discover is that I am *and*: a collage, a living, breathing paradox made of opposites and similarities, put together in a configuration that is entirely and uniquely me. The quote that gives me most peace is from the Torah. When Moses asks the Unspeakable Name of the Hebrew G!D, "What do I tell them your name is?" the answer is *"Eheyeh Asher Eheyeh"* — "I will

And: Building a World of Connection through Jewish Mystical Wisdom

be who I will be." I am a survivor, organically evolving based on my need to choose life. My brain, like yours, has a neuroplastic quality that allows me to learn new skills and information, even at this age. Scientists are proving that we are dynamic lifelong learners, and this book is how *I* do it.

I now am telling my clients and friends to join me on my mission to de-*but* the world. I hope you learn and grow from reading my entries, as I have. We do live an *and* life. Try it.

December 2012
Kislev 5773
Port Royal, SC
moon rising

2007

Friday, September 7, 2007

Step One

LISTENING

Listening to the text of my life has become very important. As I listen, I have been learning how to trust myself while encouraging a deeper relationship with myself. I am practicing learning how to love me. Only my G!D loves me so unconditionally, and even that is still hard to believe. No one else will hear what is in my head unless I speak it out loud. The Society of the *Vav* is what I heard, savored, and played with in my head and in my journal. Now I want to share and help her grow. I do not want to be the only one to nurture her.

Last spring was the first time I spoke the phrase out loud. I was in Jerusalem with my grandson Ashby for the March of the Living, and was invited to Shabbat dinner as a guest of my mystical Judaism teacher, Sarah Schneider, and some of her other students. I was surprised at the excited reaction when I mentioned the Society of the *Vav*. I did not know what to do with their response. These women are smart, educated, energetic: What was it about this phrase that excited them? They wanted to know more. As do I.

So I have put some of my musings down to share. I do this with great excitement and trepidation. I am open to all the possibilities. Of one thing I am sure: This society will be a collection of those who believe in listening deeply and trusting themselves.

Connecting Heaven and Earth — Living One Life

Leadership and meditation go together like hand and glove.

As a coach of middle and upper managers/leaders, I listen to the text of peoples' lives and try to help them make the world a better place for themselves and others. As a rabbi, I am trained in reading the Torah, never settling for the superficial, believing in the intuitiveness of the Hebrew language, and thinking through, going deeper than what appears on the surface. I love the Hebrew letters and find them a source of great wisdom.

And meditation saved my life. I learned to be able to live with myself, with less verbal self-mutilation. Meditation and mindfulness practice have allowed me to broaden my perspective on my life and the world, and to be kinder to others and myself. I believe everyone is a leader and has the responsibility to learn how to be his or her own teacher so we can learn to trust ourselves, trust the process, and treasure ourselves. Meditation and mindfulness practice support that path.

Teshuva is a Hebrew word that means "return" and "repentance." It is used to describe the right of all people — as in free will — to notice where they are in their life and to make "turns" to bring them back into alignment, because we are often getting distracted from the life we "took birth for." I have heard Ondrea Levine write about that phrase, and I am often wondering what my soul took life for. On a meditation retreat at the Insight Meditation Society in Barre, MA, I heard Sharon Salzberg, a co-founder, say that meditation is the practice of returning. The simplicity of the concept has remained with me and is aligned with the Hebrew wisdom teaching of *teshuva*.

I often use these biblical texts as intentions for mindfulness:

- We do not know how we are to serve YHWH until we come there (Exodus 10:26).
- "Where are you?" G!d asks Adam (Genesis 3:9).
- And G!d was in this place and I, I did not know (Genesis 28:16).

The idea of using the letter *vav* when talking about leadership evolved from several sources:

- having an iPod and digital recorder
- noticing my aversive response to hearing the word *but*
- knowing that life is continuous and dynamic, always changing
- the letter *vav* placed at the beginning of a word means *and*

Why the iPod and digital recorder? I noticed that these high-tech, for-the-masses instruments don't have an on-off button — they only have a hold button. I knew there was something beyond the superficial reason for this, so I allowed my mind to contemplate it. What I decided is that we only pause life, we never really stop it. So why lie or deny reality?

Whenever I hear the word *but*, my body reacts in an uncomfortable, visceral way. The word *but* negates anything that comes before it. I was taught by one of my teachers never to throw anything out, that every moment and every piece of data is important. So if everything matters, we have to deal with everything. Then my mind wandered to using the word *and*. I also noticed that when others or I use the word *but*, we often are saying something negative. We use *but* to indicate a feeling of being lost, creating a stop sign to an idea, or just giving up. I am often full of hope and usually looking for how to do something, especially if it is an idea that rings true to me. So when I hear, "What do you mean we cannot do that?" then I need to pause. I am trying not to throw out any part of my life or piece of information when moving into problem solving, even when I do not like it.

In the Hebrew language, *vav* means "hook." Much is written about the *vav* and its many usages and meanings in the Hebrew language. In relationship to the Society of the *Vav*, when you place the *vav* in front of a word, one common translation is *and*.

Life is continuous and dynamic and it is all about transitions, moving from one role or stage to another. In Exodus, Moshe asks the Divine, "What do I call You?" and the reply translates as, "I am what I am" and "I will be what I will be." Consistency and emotional safety are very important for a mind that thinks linearly. If you say you are going to do something, then I expect you to do it. How can I learn to trust someone to be honest? Can I be honest with myself or with you? My daughter Ilana once asked me to set all the clocks in my home and car to the same time so that I would not lie. I had never thought of it like that, and I changed all my clocks to reflect the correct time and my core value of being consistent and honest.

Circumcising the Heart

In coaching sessions, when I ask middle and upper managers how they protect their heart, a few ask why you would want to do that. The majority would describe how they protect their heart by distancing, placing it in a box, creating a wall around it. The heart lies in the middle of the body and is called the energy center for equanimity and beauty. It is an important organ to teach us how to hold everything, even the things we do not want to know.

Spiritual Practice

We do not live alone in the world. In *The World is Flat*, Thomas Friedman reminds us that with current technology we are connected and on an equal playing field with people around the world. Quantum physics informs us that our purpose in working in one place may have an effect in some entirely remote place on the earth. It is essential that I begin to think that my work has a bigger purpose and that I, or my ego, only think I know why I am here. Bringing to consciousness the fact that we need each other and we are all connected is what the popular culture and faith-based writings are stressing. In their classic, ground-breaking book *Presence*, Peter Senge and others write that if we listen to everything, life is a process, a never-ending linking of events.

From leadership literature I interpret that we are all leaders, and from Torah I read that we are all a kingdom of priests. Therefore, we are responsible for the care of the earth as well as the sky — what we can see and what we cannot and everything in between, including emotions and thoughts.

The letter *vav* is the sixth letter in the Hebrew alphabet and the third letter of the tetragrammaton, the four letters of the unspeakable Hebrew name for god. In mystical Hebrew wisdom writings, the Kabbala, there are many *sefirot* or divine emanations through which the Divine is revealed. The *vav* relates to six of those *sefirot*, that align with the torso, from shoulders to groin. The names of the six *sefirot* are *chesed, gevura, tiferet, netzach, hod,* and *sod*. *Vav*, which also means "hook" in Hebrew, has the energy intelligence of interconnection and unification; it is the symbol of completion, redemption, and transformation.

In working with energy for healing, the practitioner will focus above and below the affected area. The area above the torso, the neck, is the *sefira* called *da'at*, whose attribute is a focus on communication and paradox.

In *The Opposable Mind*, Roger Martin, dean of the Rotman School of Management at the University of Toronto, writes about paradox. He describes the quiet leader who must build partnership with opposing views and co-create a solution that raises the productivity of all to the highest potential. In Judaism we live with lots of paradoxes: believing in a G!D that has no physical form, and reading phrases in the Torah such as "walking into the sea on dry land" or "seeing the sound." To think nonlinearly, one must be able to hold all the information and not throw one piece of data out. The *and* — in Hebrew, the letter *vav* — helps to speak and embrace the language of paradox.

Several years ago, I led a study group that focused on leadership and meditation, which I see as interdependent — leaders must be able to sit still, focus the mind, and listen to arrive at an alignment with their head and their heart. For the workshop, I created a handout based on various text sources: leadership, mindfulness, and Judaism. Below is a list of leadership characteristics and scriptural citations that can be used to focus on during a meditation practice.

Piety: Take your shoes off your feet, the place where you are standing is holy (Exodus 3:5).
Remove anything that holds you firmly in one place so you can embrace new information that supports your becoming your authentic self.

Tenacity: It is not your duty to finish the work, and neither are you at liberty to neglect it" (Pirke Avot 2:26).
Stay focused and true to your intentions, despite the challenges.

Humility: And you shall be to Me a kingdom of priests and a holy nation (Exodus 19:6).
We live life doing the work in partnership with the Divine.

Consistency: The entire purpose of our existence is to overcome our hurtful habits (Vilna Gaon, commentary to Mishlei 4:13).
Being human involves being aware of the mind's suffering; being kind to our self and others involves integrity and knowing you are good at your core.

Compassion: Circumcise the foreskin of your heart and be no more stiff-necked (Deuteronomy 10:16) and God will circumcise your heart (Deuteronomy 30:6).
Being aware of how we protect our heart and removing the covering allows the light in and our inner light out.

Service to Others: You shall not oppress your neighbor, nor rob him ... nor do him wrong. The stranger who lives as a foreigner with you shall be to you as the native-born among you, and you shall love him as yourself (Leviticus 19:34).
Learning to honor the fact that we are interconnected, that what we do to others influences us as well.

These intentions came primarily from studying these writings:

- *Coming to Our Senses: Healing Ourselves and the World Through Mindfulness*, by Jon Kabat-Zinn
- *Meditation and the Bible and Jewish Meditation: A Practical Guide*, by Rabbi Aryeh Kaplan
- *From Sanctuary to Boardroom: A Jewish Approach to Leadership*, by Hal. M. Lewis
- *Society of the Vav: The Sixth Hebrew Letter as Metaphor and Paradox*, by Tzipi Radonsky
- *Mindful Jewish Living: Compassionate Practice*, by Jonathan P. Slater

8:49 AM

Sunday, September 9, 2007

Step Two
BE HUMBLE

Shivering Heart

This is an update, day of the evening of *Rosh Chodesh Cheshvan* 5770. Today I would write about the Society of the *Vav* differently. I can see that I am changing and growing as my perspective is broader. I would support what I had written yesterday, and today I would have more words to support this as I study *musar*, a Jewish ethical movement whose goal is to help release the light within the soul. I began my study with the first *midda* ("ethic"): humility. I am aware of holding the tension that my shyness does not serve me and it is not all about me. I am practicing holding the two opposites, being humble and being great, as within Hebrew wisdom this is possible.

This is a work in progress — learning about how to be humble — and therefore I am not sure how to write about it. I am sure it is an important part of the process of being a leader who can make the world a better place.

So what does this have to do with paradox and meditation and leadership? The coach in the movie *Hoosiers* told his star player, who loved to make those three pointers from outside the key, "Pass the ball three times before you shoot." Enable your impulse control. Work together — it is not just about me.

We need each other in this huge task of healing the world and making it a better place. I need you and I need all the parts of me, too.

9:11 PM

Tuesday, September 11, 2007

INCLUSION

Inclusion seems to be a catchword lately: inclusive community, let us not leave anyone out, make sure everyone is heard.

Perhaps the Society of the *Vav* is a similar venue.

In meditation I try to notice everything and yet not get caught by any thought, feeling, emotion. I am noticing and letting go as all of life is changing; if I hold on to any one piece, I will miss out on the next that arises.

When I do not let the hold button keep the mind in one place for too long, then I do not suffer too long, and I am allowing the natural state of being of my soul — joy — to arise. I find that smiling is so much more freeing than the seriousness of how I started writing down these words.

So what makes this Society of the *Vav* so important to write about if everyone else is noticing the importance of inclusion? Perhaps she is another element to help us awaken to the thought that we need each other. The Great Ari, Rabbi Yitzchak Luria Ashkenazi, lead a small group of followers in the study of the Kaballa, mystical Hebrew wisdom texts, in the 16th century. If he is correct and there is not one moment in time that is like another — and therefore we are each unique — then each of us is necessary in repairing the world, and each of us carries our unique spark to brighten the world.

5:28 AM

Wednesday, September 19, 2007

LOVE YOURSELF, SHE NEEDS YOU!

Graffiti from women's stall, Denver airport

Blessings of Awareness

Several years ago on a trip home from a very holy visit to Boulder, CO, I found this note stuck on the back of the door in a bathroom stall at Denver airport.

I believe there are no accidents and that this was a message for me and everyone else who saw it. I know it is a universal message, and it is up to the perceiver to discern what the words mean to them. That is my job: to figure out how to uncover my heart and let me in. The Buddhist writer and poet Stephen Levine writes that letting yourself back into your heart is how we heal.

I frequently find myself giving to or caring for someone in my community or family. I am realizing that is often easier than giving attention to myself. I am trying more to be the receiver than the giver in relationships. I am practicing with my daughters, Andrea and Ilana, to let go and see them as the capable, strong, independent young women they are, able to care for themselves and their families. I do not have to tell them how to do it, just to be there when they need me. Most people I know take very good care of themselves. The piece for me to remember is to include myself in the category of who I care for.

Spiritual Challenge

I can always open my heart and let myself in just a little bit more. I am always surprised by all that fits within this little organ that sits in the middle of my universe.

The *vav* reminds me that there is always an opportunity to come home to your heart.

Spiritual Practice

One way to do that is to have more fun. I joined the museum so I can go anytime. I take time to listen to my heart and give her what she wants: food, rest, laughter, fun, friendship.

Treating myself as if I were my own lover, friend, neighbor, child, spouse is one way of creating a balance in my life and not leaving me out of getting attention-love that I need. I whine less, too.

11:51 AM

Monday, September 24, 2007

Step Three
SETTING INTENTIONS

Several years ago I had the thought that setting goals was not getting me where I needed to be. I spoke this out loud to a friend I admire, and she agreed. I decided I needed to listen to what has been referred to as an inner sense of knowing. I did not realize I had just begun a learning curve process.

In Hebrew wisdom the word *kavana* — intention — is given much power by the sages. They taught that setting an intention creates reality, what we want to happen. Intention has become important in my life. I have been testing to see if, when I set an intention, it really does happen. In the documentary, *What the Bleep Do We Know!?*, Dr. Joe, one of the physicians, talks about setting intentions and then checking at the end of the day to see if they happened. It is a way of checking if I am in the rhythm of my life.

I set intentions by listening to the voice of my heart and my body. Some may call it intuition. The goals I set come from my head. Intentions come from within me. The goals I set are often externally driven. Of course, this may be too general a statement. I have been practicing setting intentions first, and then see the ease in which the goals evolve. Most often intentions are not measurable and the mind needs completion, checking off lists or getting external validation.

When I take the time to be still and listen deeply, I draw on information that energizes and moves me forward. When I take the time to be introspective and look at my life from a distance, I can begin to see my life reflecting what is already important to me. I just have to pay attention to my life.

Protecting the Heart

Twice in the Bible it is written to "circumcise your heart." The first reference is a command; the second says the Divine will remove the covering of your heart. I wonder, why two times? Perhaps, many of us walk around bandaged up in order to protect our heart and keep us emotionally safe. In his book on *musar*, Alan Moranis writes that circumcising the heart is the beginning of a spiritual initiation.

When I protect my heart I am not able to access its wisdom and make decisions for my life that could make the world a better place. I am not relying on my true self that rests in a higher place. I am not as creative, spontaneous, or lovable.

Some of the people I am reading lately — Jerry and Esther Hicks, *The Law of Attraction*; Steve Siebold, an inspirational speaker on thinking like a millionaire; Rosamund and Benjamin Zander, leadership consultants who focus on possibilities; and those who write and teach about David Cooperrider's Appreciative Inquiry — have all noted that the power of emotions and their relationship to beliefs and values are the key drivers for getting work done. I am seeing that by setting intentions based on my beliefs and values, I am brought to a higher purpose.

When I set goals without intention, I do this from the mind that is cut off from the heart. I am not paying attention to the body, the feelings, and the wisdom that inform me what is important. I am also not using my whole brain, but just the right side that makes analytical, linear decisions. It is useful to have a *mochin de'gadlute* — a big mind, a spacious mind — to broaden consciousness, to be more inclusive and mindful of all the elements.

Why am I here? What is the purpose in coming to work? I come to work for many reasons: to get a paycheck, because I like what I do, to learn, to enjoy the camaraderie of the workplace and connect with community. I come to have fun. I want to be energized. I want to play cooperatively with you. I want to be stimulated. I want my life to have meaning. I want to be my authentic self and be accepted for being me.

Goals are set and completed in the physical world of doing. Intentions are set and carried out through being aware of the emotional world, the world of thought and Spirit. To be continued…

4:03 PM

Tuesday, October 2, 2007

GATES OF TEARS AND *TESHUVA*

Close-up of rose with bud

Life, birth and death and everything in between, is dynamic and continuous.

Hebrew wisdom teaches that the Gates of Tears are always open, as is our opportunity to do *teshuva* — return to our true self and G!D.

Are the Gates of Tears only for tears of sadness and hopelessness?

Can they be tears of joy of coming home? Can they be both? Remembering Hagar in the desert, I ask, "Does one bring us to another?"

Perhaps we cry out of fear, loneliness, and sorrow, and the result is *teshuva*, returning to the path and a coming home to *emet*, the truth, and realizing we are at One-ment with our G!D all the time.

Perhaps that is experiencing a *zivug*, a holy relationship, as Rabbi Joseph B. Soloveitchik writes of in *Lonely Man of Faith*: G!D was lonely for us as we were experiencing our loneliness.

So I will cry, whine, and emote all my feelings. G!D willing they are the path to the open Gates of Tears, to joy in my heart and being consciously aware that I am home.

8:58 AM

Tuesday, October 2, 2007

BEING ONE, *DEVEKUTE*

Banyan trees, West Palm Beach, FL

Being one means we are never separate
   My yearning is about joy not pain
Being one means physical distance is an illusion
   So why let the mind win?
Being one means today is yesterday
   was tomorrow
Being one means I am you and you are I
   How can I ever doubt Your love for me or mine for you?
Being one means space allows us to be
   Forever young, old, born again into me
Being one means treating me as I treat You
   With patience, love, curiosity, and as not the enemy

⌨ **9:02 AM**

Wednesday, October 24, 2007

Including Me on the Daily to-Do List

Stone sculpture of praying woman, Yucatan, Mexico

I read a book recently and many others are also laughing and learning their way through it: *Eat, Pray, Love* by Elizabeth Gilbert, a woman's guide to everything.

The other day I recommended the book to a client. As I said the title, I began to think of the words as a mantra, and I offered this idea to my client. Now I put eat-pray-love on the top of my daily list as a must-do. I see this as a way of including me in my day.

Eat by filling myself during the day with delicious, nutritious, fulfilling experiences so I am satisfied in all four worlds. Even when I watch the news I am living in this world, not avoiding the pain of others.

Pray by being grateful for each breath and for the others who may be in a narrow place. Take time to meditate on the 13 attributes of G!D found in the book of *Exodus*, healing words that reflect some of G!D's virtues, like kindness, eternal patience, and compassion. And I remember to bless each morsel I place in my mouth and be grateful for the ability to walk, talk, think, and release from my body, mind, and heart everything that I do not need to carry with me.

Love, which brings a smile to my face. Surrounding myself only with love inside and out can relax me into the moment, instead of leaning forward into the next. My mother was watching me read at her table the other day and commented how happy it made her to see me sitting so upright. So all this practice may be working. *Halleluya!* And may everyone be so blessed!

Blessings of the *Vav*

Including you in your life is being soul-full.

6:36 AM

Thursday, November 1, 2007

So, What is a Vav?

In the teachings of mystical Hebrew wisdom, it is written that each letter of the Hebrew alphabet has an energy intelligence that brings with it a spiritual essence and hidden meaning that has a power to transform. *Vav*, the sixth letter, has the energy of completion, redemption, and transformation (*The Wisdom in the Hebrew Alphabet*), as well as connection and unification (*The Inner Meaning of the Hebrew Letters*). For me, the *vav* demands that I look at everything in terms of relationships from all perspectives. And that is my definition of being spiritual, knowing I am in relationship with everything, human and nonhuman, for everything is G!D.

6:33 AM

Thursday, November 1, 2007

Organizational Coaching: Living "We Need Each Other"

This is a work in progress.

I am trying to live one life. To walk my talk and live my values. My father, of blessed memory, had a favorite comment: "We need each other." He said it at *shul* when he was president, he said it to his granddaughters, and he said it to me. That was his legacy. There is a sign at the end of the community where my parents lived: "Be safe — we need each other." I like that.

In my studies of mystical Judaism and other faiths, a core concept is that we are all connected, we are one. In quantum physics, a butterfly's wings in one part of the world can cause a typhoon in a place 180 degrees away. Barbra Streisand and Cher sing that all hearts are connected. I am getting this information from all sides. And now I am reading *The Power of Appreciative Inquiry* by Diane Whitney and the concepts behind the idea of creating conversations across boundaries in *The World Cafe* by Juanita Brown and David Isaacs. Pieces of the puzzle are beginning to find each other and match my own sense of what is right.

I was in individual counseling for many years. My parents refused to go for various reasons. Years later I had a practice in individual counseling, and it was most inspiring and energizing when I worked with couples because I could see change happening. Now I do executive coaching one-on-one with clients. It works — and it really works when the individual is a CEO who can make organizational change. No matter how large or small, any change is important when peace of mind and heart happens, even for a moment. The world is going so fast, and we are too often living the illusion of separation and fear before connectedness and love.

In the Hebrew tradition the sages speak that the soul takes life to heal the tears in the fabric of the world, and each soul is unique, so it has a special offering to the larger picture.

Organizational coaching moves beyond individual coaching to live the servant leadership concept of, "It is not just about me, it is about us." It is an evolution in which the community that is made up of individuals can get a collective message through the venue of collaborative conversations. We need to go back to the original concept of councils where people in the tribes sat around and discussed the community's needs.

10:18 AM

Tuesday, November 27, 2007

THE MYSTERY
OF THE CARDS

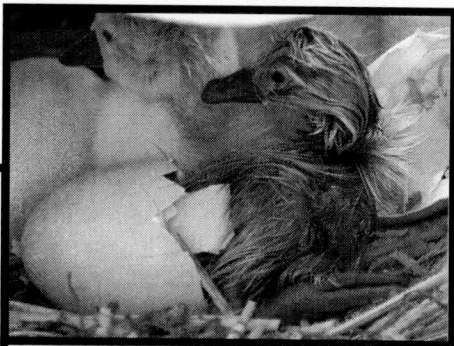

Center for Creative Leadership Visual Explorer cards: children in semi-circle and chick coming out of an egg

Who would imagine that the images would evoke such emotional responses that they would bring tears, conversations never dreamed in a coaching session, and clarity and validation of goals? I usually use the Visual Explorer cards — a deck of image cards created at the Center for Creative Leadership, a non-profit education and research facility in Greensboro, NC — at the end of a session, because I feel if the client connects an image with a goal it might mean more than the words themselves. I am always hoping for an intention to appear, a symbol that reflects an emotion, a private thought or connection to core values that is attached to the outcome, in contrast to a goal that is more in the physical world of doing.

Playing Hardball with the Boys

She was a member of a leadership-training program for women. The role she played was highly visible in a male-dominated profession and she wanted to "play hardball with the boys." Yes, this is a direct quote. I remember her as an attractive, tall, white woman with broad shoulders, married with one son, who was her most proud accomplishment. On paper she was enthusiastic and energetic about life. In person she appeared tired and pensive. By the end of the session she admitted that her Catholic upbringing had led her to believe and act that women needed to defer to men or anyone who wielded power. There was some cognitive dissonance in relation to her ambitious nature. When she picked the card that had five young boys in a semicircle with their backs to the camera and a young girl on the end, she was shocked. She paused for a few minutes, then said, "I guess I already am playing hardball with the boys, and maybe I need to act with that attitude." She later emailed to say she had gone to speak with her boss, a man, and asked for more challenges. And he offered her what she wanted.

When I contacted this participant to ask her to read the above for accuracy and to fill in the gaps, she wrote: "When I pulled the card, I first saw the young girl and then realized that the group around her was all boys. As you indicated, I was shocked about this — based on our conversation about my desire to play hardball with the boys. The other thing that struck me was that the situation depicted could have certainly been a group of kids playing ball, with one girl joining the boys. I felt an instant connection to the card, and yes, was very happy to get a copy of it. As it is on my vision board on my desk, it is a reminder to me of you, our conversation, and my desire to play hardball with the boys."

The Changing Eye of the Perceiver

He was at a crossroads in his life. All he had worked for had been accomplished, and he was no longer energized by his work. He was confused about where to go next, and was participating in a leadership program to help him become the leader that the larger community needed. He had spoken to few about his dilemma. This is what he wrote a year later: "When we sat at the Center for Creative Leadership, you showed me cards. I picked one with a newly hatched duckling. At the time, all I could see was fear of the world. Today, because of the process that you helped initiate, I reconsider that picture and realize that it is about rebirth, and about the excitement of possibilities that come with experiencing the world anew. And for those gifts, I thank you for being among those I consider my *rebbeim*."

The Missing Link

For an hour and 20 minutes of the hour and a half we had together, we worked on building rapport and deciphering the results of the surveys the young man had taken. The 26-year-old white man retained a flat affect. He did not look happy. His company believed in him enough to send him for a three-day training program, and he was still lost, unsure what he needed to do. I did not see any emotion until I gave him the cards and asked him to shuffle them any way he wished. He immediately became animated, appearing at home with the deck. He enthusiastically responded to my request by being firm and playful with the cards. I asked him how he had learned how to do this so well. He said that when he was eight his grandfather had given him specific training in the art of card handling. I do not remember the goal, but the card he picked was again the group of young people coming together. He named the picture *friendship*. "How does this relate to work?" I asked. He said he had no friends there. I asked what kind of friend he is outside of work, and he responded, "Kooky outside of work and serious and stern at work." In the few minutes left, we conversed about this challenge and what he could do to perhaps become more integrated.

Perspective of the Observer

I was curious about meeting with the 46-year-old woman. In the bio she completed before attending the leadership development program her company had sent her to, she responded to the question, "Have you ever experienced any violent or traumatic experiences, like war or accident?" with, "Growing up in a mixed-race family in the '60s during the Civil Rights Movement." When we met I saw a tall, elegant, beautiful black woman. She met my eye contact and questions with direct, confident assertiveness. When she pulled from the deck a black-and-white photo of a dandelion clock, her first comment was, "I see everything in black and white." This dropped us into a deeper conversation that confronted racism, religious prejudice, and sexism. This is the kind of coaching that soothes and massages the soul.

Afterthought

It does not matter whether the participant is male or female, extrovert or introvert, high need for control or easygoing. They all participate without much encouragement. The cards reflect a part of them and give them a metaphor that months later can remain with them. When I asked if they would like a copy of the card, almost all replied *yes* with enthusiasm that sounded like, "Of course, what a silly question" — not wanting to leave a piece of their self behind!

10:07 PM

Friday, November 30, 2007

Protecting the Heart at Work

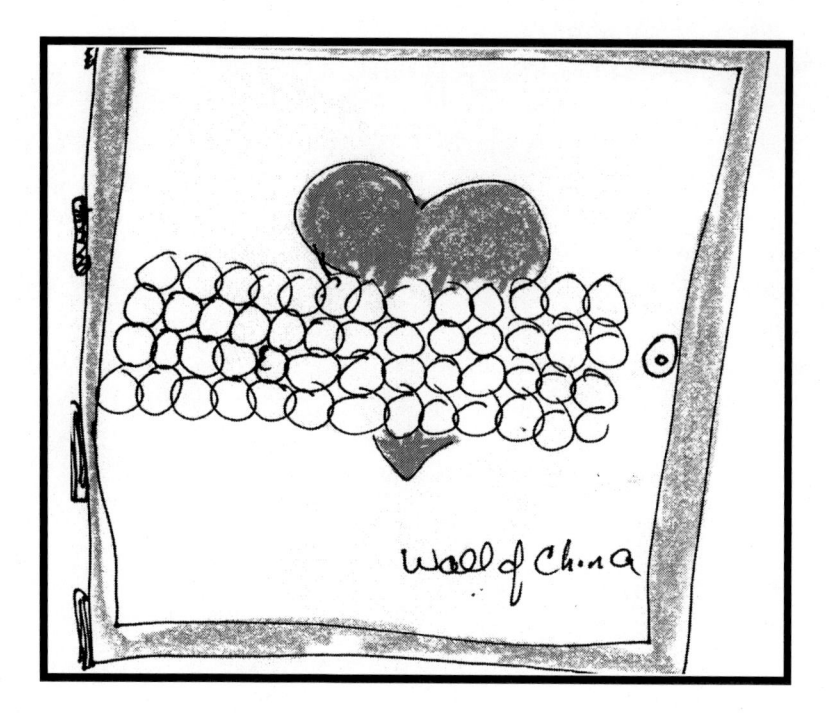

A Heart Behind a Wall

Blessings of Being Awake

There was a period of time several years ago when I began asking my coaching clients, "How do you protect your heart at work?" Of the many I worked with, only two responded, "Why would I do that?" The rest were willing to make me a picture.

Blessings of Spiritual Challenge

I have been known to spontaneously self-disclose that my heart's default is *closed*. This awareness arose in my early 40s during a therapy session, when I realized that I protected my heart with a wall of China. The wall had one ladder to get out and a few gates that only swung out, and each gate had bells to alert me when someone tried to get in. I even drew my heart in various poses of protection.

I am making light of a very serious matter. I believe that when my heart is protected, my productivity is decreased. I am expending too much energy keeping myself emotionally safe to function at my highest level of good. A Chinese herbalist said I was controlling my passion.

As a rabbi I also know that the heart is assumed to have a cover over it. Why else would there be two times when the phrase "circumcise the heart" is referred to in the Torah? We are also asked to walk before G!D with a pure heart, one that is uncovered.

The pictures that were drawn during coaching sessions ranged from boxes that you could not see into, to barbed wire. One builder gave me the name of the specific cement blocks he used. One woman placed her heart on a hill far away from everyone she worked with. I asked what was in the heart that needed protecting, and often people could not tell me. Others had elaborate stories.

The work of HeartMath Institute, an organization researching heart intelligence and stress management, confirmed my deepest concerns. The heart and brain are connected, and when the heart is full of emotion, the brain is confused and cannot always make clear decisions.

Blessings of Spiritual Practice

The first person I asked to make me a picture in a coaching session is the most memorable. A young man born in Vietnam, he and his family were boat people, having survived their escape over water. His first love was architecture, and he took to making the picture with ease. First he drew a heart with a black pen. Then with a yellow felt-tip pen he drew long strokes of what looked like rays of light from the heart, all the way around. He was a happy person, and so grateful for his gifts. Throughout the week he had been a participant the trainers and coordinators were glad to have in the group. At the conclusion, he looked back at his picture and noticed that at the end of the yellow rays were silhouettes of people around his heart. "This is how I protect my heart," he said, "with all the people who have helped my family and me." As we left the room, he gave me his business card on which he had handwritten "human being" after his name.

As I prepared to begin my training to become a rabbi, I saw myself as circumcising my heart in order to enter into a covenantal relationship with my G!D. Recently, I read the writings of Alan Morinis, who wrote in the introduction of *Everyday Holiness: The Jewish Spiritual Path of Mussar* that "circumcision of the heart is a metaphor for spiritual initiation, having an open, sensitive inner life." Now I see that when I noticed I protected my heart, I was simultaneously beginning to remove the covering, deepening my relationship with the Divine.

A good teacher models what she teaches. I notice when I lie, when I withhold information, and when I am shy. This noticing helps me stay awake and conscious, and not let old patterns keep alive the illusion that I am not safe, or cannot take care of myself, or am not connected to everything else. I also notice when I laugh out loud, let tears fall, and move slowly into a difficult conversation. Paying attention and then accepting what is — without judging — is helping me to feel a bit more emotionally safe in the world, and to be a human being. I remember when my spiritual director said that being in relationship meant sometimes I would be hurt by how angry I was. I had learned to live a life of protection so I would not get hurt. Protecting my heart made me safe, and made me miss out on experiencing lots of emotions. So slowly I am removing the coverings of my heart, making mistakes, and not making excuses — only learning what it means to be a leader. Thank G!D for the *vav*; all of my life experiences matter and make me who I am today, like my client who drew the heart with rays coming from it.

11:35 AM

2008

Tuesday, February 5, 2008

WE ARE ONE

Banyan trees, West Palm Beach, FL

This morning I sent a love note to my cousin and his fiancé to welcome her into our family and to wish them congratulations on their commitment to each other. I chose this picture because the tree reminds me of connectedness, that we are all one. I wanted her to feel welcomed by me into the family, because I am now the oldest cousin.

I took this picture years ago when I was visiting my parents in South Florida. I am fascinated by the banyan tree, which keeps growing up and out, putting down roots and then limbs, a continual process of evolving through nurturing itself. The banyan is a work of art. Every part of the tree is closely connected with each other. It seems as if there is no avoidance of intimacy. When I think of my family, of being that close to them, I feel a bit claustrophobic. Maybe that is why there is comfort in living hundreds of miles away from each other. I am curious about this feeling of not having room to breathe, the closeness I want to run away from. And this is the picture that I sent to welcome a new member of our family. Was I also saying *beware?*

I think I would like to try living like the banyan, which seems to have no fear of not enough-ness, perhaps knowing that there will always be enough room for me to spread my wings and build my nest, enough love to fill my heart to keep her open, enough attention to feel special so I can enjoy the limelight, enough acceptance of my uniqueness to nurture me, and enough time to be alone to nurture my soul that loves silence.

My name means *bird* in Hebrew, and perhaps this is a time to consider building a nest and a relationship with the banyan tree. She probably has lots to teach me about breathing in close spaces.

12:20 PM

Wednesday, February 6, 2008

WALKING THE WALK

Finishing the ING Miami Marathon, January 2007

Several years ago I was sitting on the subway in DC and my eyes caught the information for the DC Marine Marathon. As I read, a well of emotion began to rise and tears formed and fell from my eyes. I have been aware of wanting to run a marathon for quite a while and yet I stopped my desires with a list of can'ts. For the past six months I have faced that list and on January 27, 2008, I walked 26.2 miles in 7 hours and 26 minutes. When I finished I was on an incredible high! I have lived almost 65 years.

When asked who I was walking for I intuitively responded, "for all the lonely people" — people who stop short of doing what their heart wants, who stop listening or try so hard to not listen and come up with every excuse why not, whose conversations are filled with *buts* and who see no love coming at them. I walked for all the lonely people, and I like to think I am no longer a member of that club. I am noticing that I no longer linger for extended periods in those thoughts; I see them and am making a choice not to suffer.

I walked for all the lonely people who drown in their loneliness, who will not reach out or cannot reach out for help. And for all the lonely people who do not reach to help others and soothe their own pain of isolation.

I walked because I wanted to prove to myself that I am the amazing woman I believe I am, and by physically doing this I will have climbed every mountain, walked across every stream, and found my dream. I found the dream. And I love walking around with my well-earned medal around my neck.

I walked for the lonely people who think they do not make a difference in the world, who yearn for love, a smile, support crossing the street, carrying the bundles upstairs, caring for their sick child.

I walked so that I no longer get caught in the illusion of loneliness. I walked because others need me to be all I can be in the world, and by healing my heart, standing strongly with my heart, letting myself back into my heart, I can make a difference and do my part in healing the world. In listening I am building a deeper relationship with the Divine and with myself, and can answer the question, "*Ayecha*, where are you?" with assuredness.

I hear the Beatles asking all the lonely people, where do they all come from? Where do they belong? I live alone, and have for more than 10 years. I am an only child. I love solitude, and many times I have battled with the feelings of drowning in loneliness. I am therefore sensitive to this feeling in the world; I see it in nursing homes, when I walk in my gated retirement community and see people looking at the ground, when people are always on their cellphones.

It helped to learn that in *Lonely Man of Faith*, Rabbi Soloveitchik wrote that when he was lonely he remembered that his God was lonely, too. Rabbi Abraham Joshua Heschel, one of the leading Jewish theologians and Jewish philosophers of the 20th century, said his feet were praying when he walked with Martin Luther King Jr. in Selma, AL, and that is just what I did. With each step I could hear my heart singing the four letters of G!D's name. The rhythm soothed and relaxed me.

In 1996-1997 I took a year to travel around the world on a solo journey. I left thinking no one would care, that I did not matter to anyone, so just go. About halfway around, in New Zealand, I began to get a grip of the truth. This thought was an illusion to protect my heart and keep me from being in relationship with all those who love me, and with myself. I discovered that I do matter. My presence, however I choose to use it, makes a difference, and I need to take responsibility for this presence. I am integrating this memory.

It is going to be all right, Cher sings. This is a song, and a walk, and a prayer for all the lonely people so they know they are remembered and are never alone. When your dreams won't come true, someone is there for you.

I know now I was never alone, am never alone, *Halleluya*. May everyone be so blessed to hold this thought under their eyelids to read when needed!

7:38 AM

Thursday, February 7, 2008

Transformation and Healing

Center for Creative Leadership Visual Explorer card: Dandelion clock

In the fall of 2007 I met a woman who would change my life and outlook. She is tall, beautiful, and her skin tone is dark. I am white, short, and a little round. While working together as coach and client, she wrote a vision of her life six months into the future that reflected on our first meeting.

During our first coaching session I was using the Visual Explorer images to access emotions and begin to build trust. Without looking at the images, she had randomly chosen a monochromatic picture of a dandelion clock. She quickly responded in a factual manner: "I see everything in black and white." Her tone of voice felt like a challenge and that a door had been opened. I walked cautiously toward the threshold.

Before she came to the leadership program, she had responded to a number of biographical questions, including, "Have you ever experienced any violent or traumatic experiences, like war or accident?" She had written, "Growing up in a mixed-race family in the '60s during the Civil Rights Movement." I took a deep breath, walked into the space she had offered me, and asked if she could tell me some stories she remembered. Stories flowed from her with vivid language. The events felt like they had happened yesterday. I listened and wept inside.

We agreed to continue our work beyond the two sessions that her company had paid for. She had started to read *The Art of Possibility* by Zander and Zander and I suggested she consider writing an essay based on their idea presented in the chapter titled, "Giving an A." She agreed to write about what life would look like by her birthday, which was six months away, after being involved in this intense coaching work.

This is what she wrote at the end of the piece she sent me:
I am no longer living in a black-and-white world.
I am part of a larger whole.
I am shaping my future.
I am free.
From her mouth to G!D's ear.

8:56 AM

February, 8, 2008

Beginner's Mind

Portrait from drawing class

Today I took my first portraiture class. A friend had recommended the class, and when I thought about the experience I got very excited. I love to doodle, and my journals are filled with fun drawings. Only lately have I tried to be less of an impressionist and more of a realist, with eye-pleasing results.

During the class I concentrated so deeply that I was not aware of anyone, just the face of the woman and the paper and my hand moving the pencil. At some point the teacher came over to me and her voice brought me back into the room. She made some comment about distance and shape, and I realized all my concentration was not getting it "right."

It was hard and I felt like a beginner, humbled by the steep learning curve that lay ahead. When I said out loud, "This is humbling," my teacher responded, "And exciting and challenging, too." She was right. I had put myself into a new situation where I was learning and I felt awkward, like a beginner. And I had a choice as to how to proceed.

I remembered telling the lama in Nepal that I was just learning Buddhism, and his response was that we are all beginners. I breathed deeply and felt more equal with him, and more able to listen. So I decided to get out of my way of being perfect, to just have fun and love the drawing I did, even if the eyes were not geographically correct.

I like consciously giving myself permission to have fun being a beginner. I wondered about my clients and how they negotiate new territory. Nothing is ever the same, each moment is unique, so laughing is essential, especially at myself. I can live a more erotic life that way.

4:03 PM

Sunday, February 10, 2008

FLOWING INTO THE WIND

Flower, Indonesia

This morning my walking partner stopped my forward motion so I could see what she saw — what I would have missed if I had stayed goal-focused. I turned to where she was pointing and saw a version of my namesake: a magnificent beauty on the edge of the water, white, still, elegant with the wind moving her tail feathers in a delicate dance around her feet. I was awestruck. As I noticed the wind's effect, I too felt the wind blowing in my face, my face caressed by my G!D.

Our family bought a small Tri-Pacer plane in the late '60s, and when I was learning to fly I was training myself to be aware of the windsock's movement and direction. Planes, like birds, must fly into the wind, must meet the oncoming draft, to be able to get off the ground. The Hebrew word for wind is *ruach*, the same name for a level of soul as well as of Spirit.

This morning I was given a gift. I slowed down, saw my reflection in another Divine creation, and remembered I can only fly with support.

Blessings of *Vav*

Going against the wind still means you are in a relationship.

7:44 PM

Tuesday, February 26, 2008

Blessings on Your Going and Coming

Energy Movement Around the Heart

There is a song I love to sing, especially on the Sabbath. *"Shalom Aleichem,"* which first appeared in print some 450 years ago, welcomes the angels and asks for their blessings when our home is peacefully ready for Shabbat, or as Rav Heschel calls her in his book *The Sabbath*, a cathedral in time of rest. I often use the final line of the song as a mantra in meditation, as the mind wanders from the aliveness of being Here. I feel a peace rolling over me, knowing that I am not alone on the travels of the mind, as I repeat the words to myself: "for the angels are instructed to guard you in all ways, and you will be protected on your going and your coming, for now and for all time."

I have also sung this liturgical poem as I sit by the bedside of a friend who is dying, and with my 83-year-old friend, who was once a Hebrew scholar, as we hold hands and walk back to her room in the nursing home where she lives. Besides enjoying the familiar melody, I love the thought of invoking the messengers of G!D's Presence wherever I go.

Each time I travel, my daughter Ilana blesses me that I should sit next to an angel. When she speaks the words, I always wonder what these angels will look like. I am hopeful and skeptical. I just returned from two weeks of travel and as I lay in bed musing on the experiences, I am very aware that at both ends of my trip I was blessed.

My first angel whirled in and sat across from me in the waiting area by the airline gate. Sensing her presence, I had to look up to see who was there. What caught my eye was the rhinestone pin on her black sweater: Hillary 2008. I smiled as I caught her eye and gave her a thumbs-up pointing to her pin. She smiled back, and we quickly moved from superficial to deeper conversation while waiting for our plane.

Hoping to follow up on our conversation, I asked for her contact information and gave her my card. I felt excited about the possibility of reconnecting, and about this new soul — a contrast to what I already knew — entering my life. What a way to start the journey; I felt energized about what else would come my way. And I was not disappointed!

On the flight back to Florida there was open seating, and I quickly made my way toward the exit-row seats, where I could have some breathing room. As I made myself comfortable, I saw a woman getting ready to squeeze into the other bus-like rows. Without a thought I invited her to join me, and she came and sat next to me. When I hang out in an airport I feel a kinship to those around me, so I began a conversation with her, and she was easy to connect with. I had rented a car to drive home, and to my delighted surprise the woman had a car and lived very close to me, and she offered to take me to my home. Our ride confirmed for me that we are more alike than different, and I again felt honored by Presence.

In a society that is becoming more driven by fear, it is imperative that I remember the world owes me nothing and I owe the world love and gratefulness for the gift of life. In this knowing, my inner home feels peaceful as I rest in the moment of timelessness and know I am blessed on my going and coming. This time I could not only feel the Presence, I could see Her variation of colors in the amazing women who are being fully alive in their life. May everyone be so blessed.

Blessings of the *Vav*

Noticing and holding the contrasting colors, emotions, and thoughts as One.

9:54 AM

Thursday, February 28, 2008

Moving onto Holy Ground

Salem Harbor, MA

Uncharacteristically, I decided that after being away for two weeks I would not jump into my typical catch-up, head down, myopic, do not stop until I am totally back into a neat, unpacked, orderly space mode — and that I would live like a millionaire, breathe, and make space to notice that I had choices. So two times on my first day home I went swimming. Each time as I sank into the water I felt held by the Divine, and breathed deeply into that awareness and smiled. Today it rained, so I chose to just take the time to sit with the sounds of water.

Blessings of the *Vav*

How often do you experience a feeling, name it loneliness, and then notice that it is only a thought attached to a feeling, and may not be entirely true?

9:40 AM

Friday, February 29, 2008

CIRCLE OF LIFE: REDEEMING THE SPARKS

Caterpillar, the Spodick family cat, Salem, MA

Here is a cheer for putting ideas out there, and if the spark is meant to be redeemed and live, then the idea will return. I have been pushing what I thought was my own agenda about the word *and* along with the word *but*. I am holding the intention that we live one life, hence the Society of the *Vav*. This phrase is a vital part of me, so anything that separates grates on me as nails on a blackboard. I see the word *but* as stopping the flow of the energy of life.

Recently I received two emails that told me the idea may hold some truth with people I am getting to know better.

From Z: *I'm finally ready to give up the job if I can't get paid more adequately and my partner is behind me 100% in this, AND (vav) have had some ideas about other venues for my teaching, leadership, and singing, so it will be good either way. It's a very vav-ish place to be, really!*

From G: *Am working with you to "de-but" the world; it seems an honorable cause.*

Like many, my ideas take form within me and when I "out" these sparks and they are heard and echoed back to me, there is a joy of validation for the journey of mattering in the world. So come on out and play! As my teacher Rabbi Shawn Zevit says, "Your shyness does not serve you."

Blessings of the *Vav*

The opportunity to begin noticing the fractals, repeating patterns, in my life and my responses — patience and impatience and everything in between — while I wait for the connections to show up. And when do I look at my life as a continuous thread I am weaving with each new experience, and begin noticing the whole weaving as if I am creating a work of art through saying *yes, and*?

⌨ **2:41 PM**

Monday, March 10, 2008

This blog was written from an imaginary perspective with a satirical tone, attempting to model the great writers such as Swift in his essay, "A Modest Proposal," and Wells in his broadcast, "The War of the Worlds." I am in awe of my chutzpa to even compare this essay's words with these great writers. Sometimes it is impossible to go head on to a topic that has great passion for me or anyone. I am desperately seeking the clarity through writing of the power of AND.

THE AMERICAN LEGACY INCLUSIVE®
DICTIONARY DENOUNCES "BUT"

Fox News update: The president of the board of The American Legacy Inclusive® Dictionary made a statement to the press today that the word *but* would be removed from its latest edition. With pressures arising from peace activists, liberal Democrats, and universalistic groups, their spokesperson said they had no other choice.

A recent poll of popular culture and Generation X found that *but* was used less than *and* as the conjunction of choice, and therefore the publishers were swayed to support the core American values found in the poem by Emma Lazarus: "Give me your tired, your poor / Your huddled masses yearning to breathe free / The wretched refuse of your teeming shore. / Send these, the homeless, tempest-tost to me..."

No one will be left out. Despite the fact that incomes are less evenly distributed than they were 20 or 30 years ago, America is still viewed as the land of opportunity. The American Legacy board wants to begin changing the way we talk so we can change the way we think. They believe, with encouragement from Harvard-based developmental researchers, that if we keep placing *but* after each statement of fact, we are creating barriers to our forward motion and maintaining America's leading edge in the free world. "We are victims of our mind that keep us small. We are ignoring our dreams and possibilities," announced the chair of Legacy's board.

The board concurs that in order to create change in the world, *but* must be replaced in each sentence so we can rise to a higher standard of problem solving. As Einstein suggested, we must use paradoxical thinking; we cannot solve our problems at the level where they are created.

The board affirmed its decision by quoting pioneering American psychologist and philosopher William James's core values of "more, more, more! is the only way to go." And in a recent sermon, the pope assured his listeners that "The heart of his God can hold an infinite amount of love — there are no buts about this."

The American Legacy Inclusive® Dictionary board met with some opposition from those who wrote multiple theses that supported the impossibility of cleaning up all the *buts*. Yet the board remained firm in its conviction that if language is going to change the world, the dictionary must be at the forefront of such change. *But is Out* is a campaign for the American Legacy Inclusive® Dictionary across all 50 states.

Skunk & Black, authors of the venerable *The Fundamentals of Style*, believe that all conjunctions are necessary in order to give people options. Surprisingly, Japan, France, Syria, and Israel all wrote letters in support of the American Legacy's decision, which has shattered Skunk & Black to the core. Using the Hebrew alphabet for support by referencing the sixth letter — *vav* — the American Legacy Inclusive® Dictionary is assured that *and* will save the world.

For reference, we included this information about the word *but*, conjunction and preposition:

1. Indicating contrast; however, on the other hand, in contrast, nevertheless, still, yet, though, on the contrary, but then, but as you see; see also *although*.

2. Indicating an exception; except, save, disregarding, without, not including, not taking into account, let alone, leaving out of consideration, aside from, with the exception of, not to mention, passing over, barring, setting aside, forgetting, omitting (to mention); see also *except*.

3. Indicating a limitation; only, only just, merely, simply, barely, solely, purely, just, no more, exactly, no other than, without.

Note: *Most of the above is true and the rest is pure fantasy by the author. And the Society of the* **Vav** *is encouraging the board of directors of American Legacy Inclusive®*

Dictionary to reconsider its decision, because whether we like but or not, it is a force to be acknowledged.

Blessings of the *Vav*

Beginning to notice with humor when you use the word *but*, when you judge the other and exclude them from your life, when you let your imagination fly free from any encumbrance and experience the joy of freedom.

⌨ *1:35 PM*

Friday, March 14, 2008

GROWING THE TREE OUTSIDE THE FENCE

Tree of Life collage

Speeding down the road on Sunday, I caught sight of a row of trees growing on the highway side of a very high fence set on a rise. The trees were equally spaced and appeared to be trimmed to perfection. The roots of the trees were proudly showing themselves, creating a distinctive contrast to the earth and fence. I thought, "Wow, a tree growing outside a fence," and kept repeating the words as I sped along, wishing I was in the right-hand lane so I could stop to take a photo, to remember the beauty I had seen and the thought that followed. When I began coming back to Judaism, Rabbi David Zeller, a mentor and friend, now of blessed memory, asked me what kind of rabbi I want to be. I intuitively responded, "one who takes down the fence around the Torah." I did not know what that meant or would look like, I only know I sensed there was a part of Judaism not being shared.

When we had this conversation I had just returned from traveling around the world, where I had exposed myself to many traditions. Reflecting on these holy teachings, I was beginning to see the richness of the tradition of my birth, and wanted to share this joy. I was like the recovering addict who had found truth, and now wanted everyone to be saved too.

Several years later I am more articulate and, I hope, more kind to myself and more inclusive; I am committed to sharing Hebrew wisdom with my world as a way of joining with other faiths in making the world a better place. Anything kept secret takes lots of energy to hold back. When I read about Christian values and Buddhist practice and Islamic teachings all in one place, and the writers rarely invoke Hebrew wisdom, I am confused. I do not understand why; I only know I feel invisible. My ego will not let me rest in that place; my soul pushes me forward.

One metaphor for the Torah is the Tree of Life, and *Pirkei Avot* (*Teachings of the Fathers*) — a rabbinic interpretation of the scriptures — says to "make a fence around the Torah."

A fence keeps out an unwanted element and protects what lies within. I often ask what is in my heart that needs protection, and what is in Hebrew wisdom that needs to be known? Will I care for what is taken out from the fence? Can I live a life in which there is no hierarchy of wisdom, where we each have our own path to coming home, where sometimes that path is woven with elements from other places? The Society of the *Vav* says *yes*, and please do it now. Several years ago in a very intuitive moment I created the Tree of Life collage. I now call it the Tree Growing Outside the Fence.

Blessings of the *Vav*

Taking a moment to have some fun, noticing with the innocence of a non-judging mind your relationship with your fence: What does your fence look like, where does it exist, what does it protect, who does it let in or keep out, and what do you want to learn? Where are the *yes, ands* in your life, and when do you stop your imagination with *yeah, buts*?

11:16 AM

Monday, March 17, 2008

BLESSING THE NAKED SOUL

Beauty in Death collage

Today I did some internal work with a dear friend who loves me. How else could I stand there naked and not be modest? *"Ayecha, where are you?"* G!D asks, and Adam replies with a history of the past. Well, that was not the correct answer, for it was only a story. We want the naked truth.

Where are you right now in real time, in your physical surroundings? What are you feeling? What thoughts are roaming in your head? Where are you in connection to your divine self?

I learned in *Loving What Is: Four Questions that Can Change Your Life* by Byron Katie and Stephen Mitchell that I cannot escape the truth; I can only gently unpack through inquiry — asking questions, carefully stripping down and uncovering the truth at the very core of your being. That is love.

The process reminds me of studying Torah, delving deeper, seeking what's hidden beneath the surface words, looking for the holy. When I began studying the Bible I found it boring until I started looking at the characters as human beings who I could be in relationship with. In getting to know them, I could get to know me.

In this month of Purim, when the hidden is revealed and Esther's coming-out saves a nation, I begin to notice my clearing-out preparation for being rebirthed. While the moon changes her face, moving us closer to the freedom of Passover, I am mindful of the work of uncovering my heart.

Blessings of the *Vav*

Welcoming home all of yourself, no matter what it looks like or how much you do not want to admit it belongs to you. The opportunity is to get to know your soul and her destiny without judgment while staying in relationship with every element of your life. Let the *vav* comfort you, as you develop a compassion for you.

4:13 PM

Sunday, March 23, 2008

Teach What You Need to Learn

Stalks in a North Carolina tobacco field

In a coaching session last week, my coach, Alan Seale, intuitively reflected to me the phrases, "You are the One" and "you are the one." I interpreted his words from my Hebrew wisdom perspective to mean I am made in the image of the Divine, holy; I am one person struggling to make a difference in the world, and to learn my purpose. I have been trying to bring clarity to my primary focus for the work I do. And I do not want to give up on the gift of these words. The phrase holds a paradox and a truth that cannot be denied. I ask myself: Are these the words of my particular soul's mission, or are they his, or is this phrase a universal truth from wherever you stand?

Whenever I am scared beyond any external control I may have over my life, I say, "*Sh'ma Yisrael Adonai Eloheinu Adonai Echad* (Hear, Israel, the Creator of all life, your God, is One). When I am dealing with the thoughts of competition or envy, I usually remember the teaching of the Great Ari, who taught that there is not one moment in time like another, so each one of us is unique. I remember then that I have a choice whether to suffer or not. What if I believed and lived "You are the One" and "you are the one" when I was not afraid, or in the middle of services three times a day while praying? I wonder what my life would be like.

When a friend was coming back to the faith of her birth, she would say the constructs over and over, and although she said it felt awkward at first, eventually she really believed that Jesus was her savior. During the last few days I have been saying "You are the One" and "you are the one" over and over again, getting to know it better and waiting for the internal "YES!" to evolve. I am getting to know the words and going deeper with the phrase, and yet I am not there yet, not even knowing where *there* is.

This morning I remembered a phrase someone once said to me — "Teach what you need to learn" — and I laughed. Of course, if I want to really get to know this phrase I must speak it out loud, remember it when I am in a narrow place and when I am in joy, and write about it until it is mine.

Identity seems to be a theme with people of my ilk, seeking who I am and what I am doing to make the world a better place. We seem to consistently forget until a reflection reminds us of the truth that we are doing good things in the world, we do have a unique gift to give, and we are more alike than different. What if each moment of consciousness reminded me of "You are the One" and "you are the one"? I am curious.

So two days after the hidden was revealed on Purim, on this Easter day when my neighbors are celebrating the resurrection of Christ, I am sitting beside them in the universe, honoring the coming of spring and the opportunity to free myself from the constraints of separateness, to experience my at-Onement and the unique gifts we — me included — bring to the world. May we use them for good.

Blessings of the Vav
Life is dynamic and continuous and inclusive.

Tuesday, March 25, 2008

Living One Life; Being a Rabbi Who Loves Her Leadership Development Work

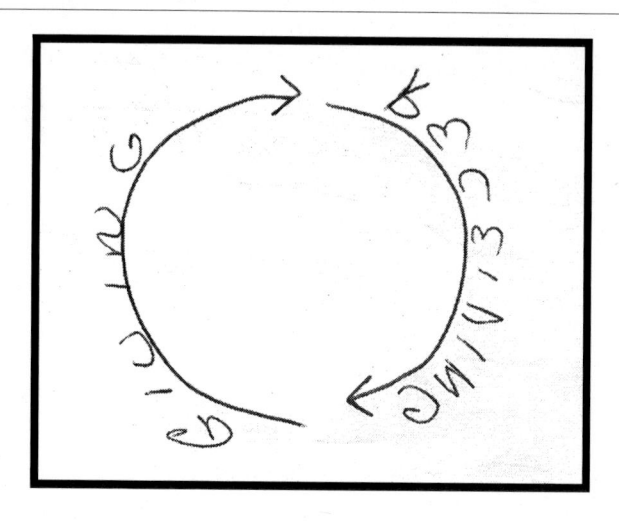

Giving & Receiving

Create Me a sanctuary and I will dwell there (*Exodus* 25:8).

When I am facilitating a small group of leaders, I usually set an intention, a deep desire of my heart, before we begin. It helps me to remember why I came to work that day. The list of intentions usually includes: having fun, laughing, and learning from each other. Collaboration is a core value, and I talk about gathering the wisdom of the group and not being the only expert in the room. After I write intentions on the board as a way of setting the tone for beginning our process, I draw a circle in two parts, with arrows facing the same direction. I label these arrows "giving" and "receiving." My hope is that the conversations among us will be rich and fruitful.

In *Zami*, African American essayist, poet, and novelist Audre Lorde's autobiography (1934-1992), the author describes herself as an only child who is like her mother and her father; she wants to be active both in the act of inserting herself into another and to be entered by another. My first reading evoked sexual thoughts and feelings. As an only child I have often wondered if I am more akin to my mother or my father, and Lorde offered me the freedom to be like both. My teacher Marc Gafni taught in our *maggid* class that the sexual only models the erotic and is not only the erotic. I have interpreted this to mean that when I am feeling totally alive, aroused everywhere, I may understand this as being sexual — and that is the mind responding to the feeling. And experiencing an erotic feeling could also mean that I am feeling the Spirit alive within me. In mystical Hebrew wisdom, a person is considered to have both a masculine and a feminine distinctiveness. The feminine essence expresses the energy of receiving and is held on the left side of the body. The masculine essence is characterized in the externalizing energy arising from the right side of the body. And the conscious awareness of the potentiality of the two coming together is the ultimate connection in making the world a better place.

Last night when my teacher, Rabbi Miriam Shulamit Ribner, taught on the feminine essence of G!D — *Shechina*, the indwelling Presence of the Divine — I felt my worlds coming together. As I am setting an intention within the small group of leaders at work for giving and receiving, I am simultaneously creating a vessel for the Divine Feminine to be within the midst of the conversation for the participants and for myself. Creativity, wisdom, and change can now be linked, bringing forth the sparks of new ideas and the potential of breaking old patterns. At least that is my expectation.

A few weeks ago that is exactly what happened. I do not know if anyone in the group would have called it holy. I did, and I knew it was different from what I had experienced in the past, and very powerful. We became one as a group supporting each other, present in our conversations and uniquely distinctive in our way of being. Some say love is a process of both giving and receiving; perhaps that was what I was feeling, what I desire from the intention I set. In being more consciously aware of what I was doing by setting an intention for the group, I could see the outcome with different eyes.

Blessings of the *Vav*

The potential to be awake and aware, to give, to receive, and to create a holy vessel of transformation all in one moment. And to experience love. After all, I learned from one of my heroes, the Beatles, that is all you need.

10:36 AM

Monday, April 7, 2008

THIS NEARLY WAS MINE

Love Coming Through the Window

Blessings of Being Awake

While walking this morning I found myself singing "This Nearly was Mine." I had heard a rendition the other night and it left a vivid impression circulating in my consciousness. In my heart I felt the yearning of Ezio Pinza singing of his lost love in *South Pacific*. "This nearly was mine," I said to myself, and wondered, "What was nearly mine? What did I miss out on, and what really is mine?"

"Nothing and everything," was the response.

Spiritual Challenge

The truth is nothing is mine, and when I get caught up in all the absoluteness of a two-year-old I can only bring myself to a very narrow place. My idea, my thought, my whatever, separates me from the world. Even the thought that I missed out on something only brings the emotion of sadness and the thought that I had done something wrong, again. As a teenage mother who still thinks her daughter is hers, this is a call to wake up to the truth that she never was mine and will always be my daughter to share with the world.

In mystical Hebrew wisdom there is a teaching that the physical world, the world of *assiya*, of doing, is perfect just the way it is. It might not be how I would want it to be, and yet this is what I got.

Spiritual Practice

So again I am given the option of noticing the feeling and choosing how to interpret the emotion, what thought to give it. Since I do not know the ending, I will just notice the feeling and wonder and choose not to prophesize. This is Nisan, the month when we honor the story of the Exodus of the Hebrews from Egypt, and I am singing another song: I am opening up to sweet surrender to the luminous love light of the One. This is mine, my heritage, my faith, my G!D.

Blessings of the *Vav*

When we hold it all and it feels too much, let it go, give it up, and be just here.

7:55 AM

Thursday, April 24, 2008

The *Vav* as a Symbol of Paradox

Vav Standing Between Heaven and Earth

There she stands, the *vav*, erect, with her little hook on top, amidst the six directions — north, south, east, west, above, and below — holding all, being the center of all there is. The *vav* connects differences that need to be held in order to appreciate the whole, for only when we know all options can we move forward and not feel caught as victims in our life.

Lately I have heard myself saying I must embrace the paradox when in conversation with people who feel confronted with a dilemma and need to choose between two options. They feel frozen in time, not liking either choice, or instead choose to check out and not even look back at what they are leaving because it is too painful.

I listen to them feeling frustration and I listen to me waiting for something to arise so I can offer another perspective. I feel what they feel and am blinded by fear, old habits locking me into a rut that has become so familiar it seems to fit perfectly. And in the silence I breathe deeply, asking, "*Ayecha*, where are you?" Somehow I am awakened and become the sixth letter of Hebrew wisdom, the *vav*, who sees in all directions. I am unlocked from whatever has held me captive, free to be clear in a vision for the next moment, and I speak what the *vav* has offered. And I see a smile or hear, "I had not thought of that," and I say a prayer of gratitude, for another life has been saved.

Blessings of the *Vav*

Being given the opportunity to take a deep breath, to live in the silence with fear, and to appreciate all possibilities, including self-love.

8:10 AM

Friday, May 2, 2008

COMING-OUT IS GETTING EASIER TO DO

Pomegranate of Love

I once asked a client to monitor when he was editing or withholding information. He used the word "appalling" to describe the amount of information he chose not to disclose. He and I are very much alike. If I got paid for how much I edit my conversations, I would be a millionaire. I do not think he and I were always like this; we learned this skill.

At 65 I seem to be blessed with an ease of speaking out information that once was too difficult to let go. Maybe I am returning to a state where I feel safe enough to handle the effects of my words. A long time ago a wise friend told me that there are three reasons one comes out or speaks freely from the heart: to push people away, to bring people closer, and to just be oneself. My intention and deepest desire is to heal the world one heart at a time by going deeper with my conversations and relationships with myself and others. Recently I heard from a friend older than I that as you age you edit less, because what have you got to lose? Hebrew wisdom might say this de-editing is a process of circumcising my heart, of removing the layers that hide the purity of my soul and redeeming the spark that is uniquely me.

Usually the phrase "coming-out" is linked with the gay community. As an advocate and trainer for making the work environment gay friendly, it is a term I am comfortable saying. Being myself is energizing, and it takes a lot of work to withhold information. As the country western song says, I still have to be awake to know when to hold information, when to say just enough, when to not be in competition, and what you need to savor just for yourself. A core teaching of Hebrew wisdom and leadership development is to know yourself. That is how building collaborative partnerships works. My self-awareness comes through being conscious of the trials and errors, deep contemplations, and writing while living in community with family, friends, colleagues, and angels who gift me with a mirror of my behavior when I dare to look.

I learned a very long time ago that if I edit my thoughts and emotions, I can be a chameleon, invisible, safe, and not rock the boat. Of course this is a conundrum, because I want to be known, appreciated, and included — and I love to be invited to have fun.

Coming-out comes in various flavors and patterns. Yesterday I self-disclosed to a client what we both knew was true and yet could have been left unspoken. My client, a Southern Baptist, was beginning to trust me — someone who would never believe that Jesus Christ is her savior and, therefore, by traditional teachings, was going to hell. I wanted us to live in that awkward place and see if we could raise each of us up to our highest good to explore this paradox. We continue to be committed to our growth.

I've noticed that in the last six months I have started freeing my ideas. First came exposing a dream that seemed to have no roots other than in my head: starting the Society of the *Vav* blog. Then I wrote about completing the Miami Marathon, walking for all the lonely people who give up on their dreams, as I have in the past. Inserting Hebrew wisdom into my leadership training, honoring my Jewish roots, was also a step in coming-out. Then I decided to write to each past and current client that I am building my practice. I can still hear the voices saying, "Why do you have to tell them that?" I feel the earth shaking under my feet while knowing that the earth is my G!D and She has got me covered.

And the internal judger still sits, guarding the gate of my tongue, testing my intention to free my soul.

Blessings of the *Vav*

There is always space to add what was left out intentionally or unintentionally when I remember it is my life I am saving.

9:02 PM

Tuesday, May 20, 2008

A Core Value: Kindness

A single rose

Today I spoke with my landlord, who will soon be my neighbor. She lives in New York, and was so appreciative of my help in caring for her condo. I began to respond with lots of words and then I stopped and said, "It is just basic kindness, Anne Marie," and tears came to my eyes.

My thesaurus states that *kindness* is synonymous with the words *caring, sympathetic, nice, gentle, thoughtful, compassionate, benevolent, humane, considerate, benign, humanitarian*.

I remembered the day we buried my father, of blessed memory: how sharp-cornered everything felt. When the funeral director softened those corners for me I felt embraced and tenderly held and was able to take a deep breath. When I thanked him he said, "It is just basic kindness," and I thought yes it is, and why is it not like breath to me?

I went to Club Med recently and was blown away by their hospitality. My heart waited for the ball to drop, the welcome to end, the warmth to cool, the generosity to shrink up. It didn't, and I was able to soak up their caring, generous, authentic spirit. By the time I left, my heart had so enjoyed mirroring their welcome that I felt as if I owned the place. I was at home in their home.

At my 45th high school reunion I was on an emotional high, having set myself up for the pleasure of being with the people who I so enjoyed in 1959-1961. Nothing could douse my spirit. During the evening one of my classmates came over to me and said, "You were kind then and you are still so kind." I don't recall anyone ever saying that about me, to me. Today I am beginning to see a pattern of one of my core values: kindness. I value that unfolding.

Blessings of the *Vav*

Going up and down the ladder of the *vav* allows me to be like Jacob's angels, who went up and then down. Each time I go up to an experience I bring back an awareness of the Divine moment and weave a distinct, unique me.

4:55 PM

Tuesday, May 20, 2008

FIND YOURSELF A TEACHER, FRIENDS

River of Light

When I first met Stephen Levine I wanted to speak with him during a break in his workshop. The line was slow as he gave personal attention to each participant, and when I came within about five feet of him I started crying uncontrollably. I had to leave the room and never got to talk with him personally. Later, I wrote him a letter about my experience and asked the questions I had not been able to ask at the workshop. He wrote back, answered the questions, and added, "You are your own teacher, trust yourself, treasure yourself, and trust the process." Every once in a while when I am starving for a mentor, I soothe myself with these words. And then I remember that in Hebrew wisdom my teacher, myself, is always there in the Indwelling Presence of G!D, *Shechina*.

Then I start thinking about all the people who teach me what I need to know and the mentors who lead me through the labyrinth of my life because they have been there first. And I smile at another moment when I chose to be kind to myself.

Blessings of the *Vav*

The fullness of one's life is in acknowledging the souls within it and the variation of choices we make. Life is not flat.

5:22 PM

Friday, May 30, 2008

ADDICTIONS

Challah and candlesticks

Addiction seems to be the theme for this week — addiction to feelings, thoughts, patterns of behaviors, addiction that causes pain and suffering, and unhealthy ways of coping with both.

I am moving to a new home that I just bought. An old pattern — avoiding a permanent home — was broken. While getting ready for the move I have not asked one person to help me; there I am stuck in the old pattern that I can do it myself, thank you very much. My thought is that, although some have offered, I am nowhere ready to direct them.

I became addicted to my thoughts, which were going 200 miles an hour as I ran from one part of my condo to the other, never completing a task. I started to pack a shelf of books and came across one that needed to be in another box so I took it to the office, where I got involved in checking my email and responding to the latest memo, then realized I was thirsty and walked toward the kitchen, stopped to relieve myself and found something on the bathroom counter that needed to be thrown out in the kitchen, walked to the kitchen to grab a snack, and saw an empty box in the kitchen that could be filled.

Looking back it was like when I was out of control and needed to be on lithium. I did not think there was another way until this morning, while I waited for the plumber to repair the flapper in the toilet tank. I could not leave as I did yesterday. Perhaps I was a bit exhausted from the running and moving all week, so I stayed in the house to finish tasks I had started. I looked at my to-do list and completed items left over from other days.

Thank G!D it is Shabbat and I choose to rest.

Blessings of the *Vav*

Sometimes there are too many ands to manage. Slowing down helps me move outside of the old patterns I am addicted to and think, discern, and be kind to myself.

5:52 PM

Wednesday, June 11, 2008

AN ARTIST'S PRAYER

Collage with dead horse head

As I move through the place I am leaving, I see details I cannot avoid. I found this prayer I had stuck up on the transom of my office/creativity room. I have had it for quite a while and could not throw it away, and in its present condition I could not take it with me. So I sat at the computer to copy it and as I read the words I knew I needed to make this poem my own, and create a new poem based on the one that an "anonymous" person had written. I was going to add my unique perspective and hopefully new energy for my new home. I think we are all artists in our own way; not quite like Bezalel, the character in the Torah who was asked to lead the children of Israel in building their sanctuary, yet who is judging? If we are all created in the image of the Divine and in Her likeness, then we are capable of being creative and doing our part to enhance the beauty of where we are.

AN ARTIST'S PRAYER

O Great Creator of All Life, Breath of our Breath
We gather Here in Your name
That we may be of service to You
And to our sisters and brothers
We offer ourselves to You as instruments
We open ourselves to Your creativity in our lives
We surrender to You our old ideas
We welcome Your new and more expansive thoughts
We trust that You will lead
We trust that it is safe to follow
We know You created us and that creativity
Is Your nature and our own
We ask You to unfold our lives
According to Your plan and let us see what we have deemed impossible
Help us to believe that it is never too late
And we can be healed and feel the connectedness with all things
Help us to love one another
To nurture each other's unfolding
To encourage each other's growth
And understand each other's fears
Help us to know that we are never alone
That we are made in Your Image and loved and lovable
Help us to create as an act of worship to You.

After I uploaded the blog, a friend read the entry and informed me that the author of the poem is Julia Cameron from her book *The Artist's Way*.

Blessings of the *Vav*

In adding our touch we are creating something new and putting our mark on the world. "Everything changes" is not a burden when we live with the possibility that with each breath we are loving our self.

4:43 AM

Monday, June 16, 2008

I Know Nothing — or at Least I Need to Pretend I Do

Collage from handmade paper, Sri Aurobindo Ashram, India

On Friday I received a message from a healer friend in Israel that she needed hands-on help with some distance work she was doing with a woman in Brooklyn. Sunday I was able to connect with the family. Not knowing how I could help, I moved in slowly, speaking openly about my limited experience with their needs and offering to do what I could to find someone locally for them. When I got off the phone I tried very hard to sit in a place of not knowing, asking for information that might lead to knowing what my part in this process was. I was aware of how the ego was playing and teasing me to be more involved, judging me for not jumping in. When a persistent idea kept coming into my consciousness, I called and offered the information to the family. As we talked, more thoughts arose that were helpful and mind-expanding for the family member I was speaking with. In the humble place of not knowing, there was space for information that needed to arise. I am in awe.

Blessings of the *Vav*

Even when I think I know what belongs after the next *and*, I must breathe deeply and allow what needs to fit the space to arise, without the desperate mind's arrogant need to fill space. I must impose impulse control and *tzimtzum* — the act of contracting to make space for another; in mystical Hebrew wisdom it is written that G!D contracted energy and light in creating the world — make space for the other. I am not alone! Another moment to act in the image of G!D.

8:05 AM

Wednesday, June 25, 2008

INTENTION: TO SAVE A LIFE

Red poppy, Old City, Jerusalem

In Hebrew wisdom we are taught the importance of the intention to save one life. In fact the poster on the wall in my friends' home quotes the Talmud: Whoever destroys a single life destroys the entire world, and whoever saves a single life saves the entire world.

I believe that I have always wanted to make the world a better place. When I was a young mother in Peabody, MA, I donated many times to the Red Cross, as I thought that my blood was the only thing I had to give.

Yesterday I worked with a woman who felt caught in the fortress around her heart. The day after our session she was beaming, no longer captured by the past. She wrote me a short note saying, "You not only saved a life, you did a *mitzva.*" A *mitzva* is a way of connecting the physical soul with the Divine soul, and being at the right place at the right time on the soul's mission and path.

When I wonder about my work as a rabbi and what impact I have on people as a healer of hearts, I will remember this moment. I remember one *erev* Shavuot when a group of women got together to study all night and told stories of their relationship with Judaism. It was a lovely evening, gentle, kind, open. When everyone was heading home, each asked to do it again; they felt connected in a new way to their roots, and that made them happy.

Today a healer asked me if I had been working with people who have so many gifts they were confused as to which path to follow. Caught in my linear, all-or-nothing, good-or-bad thinking, I limit my choices for how I will love myself and my life! We spoke of embracing and integrating our interests and living one life that is layered with passions over a lifetime; each passion feeding the other.

How can I save my life? I tell my clients that a good coach listens deeply to their voice as well as to my inner voice, and then we collaborate to help them get what they want and need. I must do that for myself, too.
Writing helps me accept myself, confident that I am embracing all of me as I create and save one life.

Blessings of the *Vav*

If the *vav* can save the world, then the *and* can save my life through including all of me, loving all of me, despite the rough spots. I am saving my life for Who knows what will come next.

11:25 AM

Sunday, July 6, 2008

Hungry Ghosts and the Grasshopper Story

Stalks in a North Carolina tobacco field

Reading Lisa See's novel *Peony in Love*, I learned that in the Chinese tradition,, people who die before completing their life's mission are called hungry ghosts. Their energy hangs around until fed and completed. In Hebrew wisdom this is called a *dybbuk*, a disembodied soul that wanders among the living, hoping for a resolution that will send its soul on its way. During this wandering the emotions related to the unfinished business of the soul remain unfettered.

While reading Jason Shulman's *Kabbalistic Healing*, I learned more about paradox and being able to hold opposites and the importance of integrating them into awareness. He suggests that being able to hold opposite emotions, like love and hate, helps to expand the world of thinking in the mystical Hebrew wisdom world known as *beria*. This act strengthens the mind to be able to live purposefully knowing the universal truth: Paradox is everywhere.

I am now calling the emotions that I seem addicted to *hungry ghosts*. I decided that if I fed them, gave them attention, perhaps they would not need to keep hanging around and distracting my energy from getting what I want.

So as I noticed the flickering of an emotion that I would have typically tossed aside, I instead started paying attention, drawing the ghosts, and naming each one: the *need-to-look-good hungry ghost*, the *never-enough hungry ghost*, the *fear-of-failure hungry ghost*, the *I want to be special hungry ghost*. Instead of tripping over them, I have decided to stop denying their presence and just feed them. One day I even made a plate of food and put it out, just as the people in See's book do.

One of my favorite parts of the Bible is what I call the Grasshopper Story, when the spies Moses sends to check out the holy land return saying there are giants covering Canaan. Ten of the 12 spies fear the giants will see the Hebrews as grasshoppers — indeed the Hebrews see themselves as grasshoppers in comparison. When G!D hears this, an immediate decision is made: No one with those thoughts can go into the holy land, and the years of wandering begin. So with the strength of a giant I am facing my hungry ghosts, feeding them and sending them on their way so I can get into the holy land sooner rather than later. Why not? Only G!D knows how much time I have on this earth, and I have too much to do to get hung up on any of these grasshopper moments.

Blessings of the *Vav*

To be clear of heart and mind, a whole picture must be viewed, including all emotions: I am sad and happy about leaving and going, all in one breath.

10:11 PM

Tuesday, July 15, 2008

NEW MOON:
AN OPPORTUNITY FOR
A RENEWAL LIFE

Tree and New Moon

The intention of the month of Tamuz is to look at things as they are. As I prepare to step into the mikva, ritual bath, and cleanse myself of the past month's experiences, I begin to think and feel what I want to cleanse myself from, and what new intentions I want to set.

This month my coaching focused on what I was missing and what in actuality I have — lots! I am *ma'ayan raz*, an eternal spring. Not that I am special in any way; this eternal spring is within everyone and we, I, just have to remember this truth.

To me, eternal spring means that I am connected to the Divine, I am never alone; whether or not my heart is innocent, uncovered, unclouded by the emotions that can constrict the natural rhythmic flow, living in the present moment and imagining possibilities.

So what do I do to remember this truth, since I do forget? I teach what I have to learn, I put me at the top of my list, I welcome and surround myself with people who are sometimes wild and crazy and do not limit their thinking, and I try to learn from them. I take good care of myself, most times, through eating what I need to keep me healthy, exercising, resting, and having objects around me that remind me of joy, love, and possibilities. I acknowledge what I know and how much more I want and have to learn. I listen to my heart. I ask for forgiveness of myself as well as others. I admit what I do not know and have forgotten. I listen to what I speak to my clients and learn from what they tell me. I look for fractals, patterns that appear in my life. I am learning that in order for a spring to continue to flow, it needs to be replenished and cleansed from all sources.

Blessings of the *Vav*

Life is an eternal spring if I choose to see it that way. I can see life as chaos, and then I can take a deep breath knowing this too shall pass and a new moment, a new moon, will arise, offering me an opportunity to begin anew.

7:54 AM

Friday, August 8, 2008

A Birth Day

Stone sculpture of praying woman, Yucatan, Mexico

When the sun rose this morning I remembered that I became a mother 46 years ago and I smiled at the gift given to me when I was not looking. I sit here now, knowing that when the sun sets in a few hours I will begin 26 hours of rest. In preparation of the visit of the Sabbath, I am taking a deep breath and patiently sitting here for just a few more minutes before I will have an opportunity to experience what Rabbi Heschel calls "a piece of the world to come." When Shabbat is over, the saddest day in Jewish history will begin; I can hear the haunting chant of Lamentations ringing in my ears and feel the universal sadness of loss and the destruction of dreams.

I am in awe that I can hold in my heart the uniqueness of each of these very powerful events and not blend them, not give them a hierarchy, not lose their impact on my life, and not try to categorize or explain them away. Each is as important as the creative project I am giving birth to today.

It has been almost 11 months since I began this blog and started looking at the blessings of the sixth Hebrew letter, *vav*. My new Israeli friend, Beenie, helped find a Hebrew name for this idea that came through me: *Agudat HaVav*, because *aguda* infers connection, and connecting to myself and others is my intention, my deepest desire. I am continuing to water the concepts without knowing where we are going, for I am building my faith in the mystery I sometimes call She, *Shechina*, In-Dwelling Presence, or G!D.

One of my daughter's fears is that she will not fulfill her mission as a mother or wife and stay in her relationship, and that she will do the same behavior that her mother displayed and leave in the middle of a run. And sometimes I have the same thought floating through my heart. Can I stay present in my life? Today, abandonment is not an option. I am not a grasshopper, as my ancestors thought of themselves. My spirit is full and large and I have the tenacity of the leader that I am.

Watering the tree sounds like such a small chore. Trust me, it is not, as distractions are rampant. My other thoughts provoked by fear are that there is not enough water, I cannot find the vessel to carry the water, where is the tree anyway, where is the water, and I am not good enough to do it. These thoughts are upstream thoughts, as Abraham speaks of, and not acceptable to this mind that I live with. I am the One who is doing the watering and I am taking my commitments seriously.

And I am watering from the eternal well of the Society of the *Vav*: This is a holographic loop — the *vav* is the tree, is the body of the Holy Name, of my body, and is *ma'ayan raz*, the eternal well, my sisterhood of friends. What a powerful image to hold as I shut off my connection to the world and contemplate rest, study, and love.

Shabbat shalom, 7 Av 5768

⌨ **3:44 PM**

Sunday, August 10, 2008

BEING INCLUDED IS LIKE BREATH TO ME

Mary K's garden, Greensboro, NC

This is a review of *Love Bade Me Welcome*, to honor Phyllis Silverman Ott-Toltz, a new friend. The memoir was written with Barbara Bamberger Scott.

"Only when a person expresses uniqueness can a meaningful joining with others occur," writes Edward Hoffman in *The Hebrew Alphabet: A Mystical Journey*, on the meanings of *vav*, the sixth Hebrew letter.

In the early '70s when I had been married a few years, my mother enrolled me as a life member of Hadassah, an international Jewish women's organization. I had married someone who is not Jewish and was living in the Bible Belt in South Carolina, and I think my mother was hoping it would help me stay more connected with the Jewish people. She was right, and I am sure she had no idea how this gift would heal my heart around my other-ness.

A few years ago I was musing through the monthly *Hadassah* magazine and in the recently published book section the words *Meher Baba* jumped out. My heart skipped a beat with excitement and disorientation. I took a deep breath: I am reading a traditional Jewish magazine — how did my outside life get here?

In the late 1990s and early 2000s I had returned to the Jewish community with the passion of a *ba'al teshuva*, one who returns. My path included studying in my local Reform community, which led me to become a bat mitzva; searching for ways to bridge my Buddhist practice with Judaism; working at Elat Chayyim, a Jewish Renewal retreat center as an intern and then two years on summer staff; and listening to my heart — which kept saying, "I want to become a rabbi" — by applying to rabbinical college and aligning myself with a rabbi who would train and ordain me.

Because Buddhist meditation had enabled my returning to Judaism by softening the covers around my heart, I wanted to learn contemplation from a Hebrew wisdom perspective to continue with my coming home. One winter when I could not make it from North Carolina where I was living to the retreat in New York, a friend recommended Meher Baba Spiritual Center (MSBC) in Myrtle Beach, SC. I was desperate for silence, and gave them a call.

MSBC welcomes guests as long as they are interested in learning about Meher Baba and his teachings. I learned that Meher Baba was an avatar living his life as a god man. The center was established in the 1940s with a gift of about 500 acres on the Atlantic Ocean. Although Meher Baba visited the center from India only one time, it holds his holiness. His devotees have created a wildlife sanctuary that was exquisitely run in the beginning by several women devotees and now is maintained mostly by volunteers. Wearing my *kippa* and asking for my silence to be honored, I was welcomed with great love and appreciation of my tradition and needs. At first I was cautious, as Baba's pictures were everywhere and I was not sure of anyone's intention. Yet the more I visited, the more comfortable I became with the acceptance and love from the staff. It was easy for me to want to return many times after that. At MBSC the teaching is to be yourself, don't worry, be happy. I found that aligned with the core teachings of Hebrew wisdom that chesed, lovingkindess, and G!D's love are eternally there and yours for the taking.

I am continually and unconsciously looking for role models — sisters who will soothe the pain of feeling different and outside the norm, and help me celebrate my uniqueness. So when I read about Phyllis Ott and Meher Baba in *Hadassah* magazine, I immediately ordered the book.

When it arrived, I stopped everything, hungry for the unknown. I was delighted to learn that Phyllis and I had many things in common. We were both born Jewish, grew up in small working-class communities around the North Shore of Boston, and both Aries. We are mothers, women spiritual searchers for the Divine, who wrestle with what it means to be and live as a Jew. Our schooling took different routes, as she found her intellectual place and artistic passion early at home, through being a graduate of Radcliffe-Harvard, and as an artist. The book is a memoir told to a friend. She and her collaborator hold nothing back, recording her life as other great painters with large brushstrokes, while giving great attention to all the details for accuracy, even the ones we wish were forgotten. *Love Bade Me Welcome* describes her transformation from a very bright, curious, "scared kid" to a brave woman artist, secure in her devotion to her mentor, Meher Baba.

Phyllis continues to live at MBSC in the home where her husband, Lynn, and their children spent several years as the only family Meher Baba allowed to live on the land. She travels, creates, and hosts family, friends, and guests who arrive at the center. Her life continues to offer challenges that keep her vital as she passes on her wisdom through mentoring others.

The next time I was at MBSC I called Phyllis and she welcomed me into her home and life, and our friendship began. In our times together she loved to interject her Hebrew wisdom heritage into the conversation, seeking validation of a memory or engaging in questioning of perspectives. I think Phyllis would be pleased as I compare her book to a *vidui*, a traditional Hebrew wisdom process of confession, a truth-telling as one prepares to die, a recounting of the stories hidden in the heart. And I do not think Phyllis Ott is ready to die; she is wanting the world to feel connected to her, and now all who read her story are joined with her in this world and eternally. May everyone be so blessed to say *heneini*, here am I.

"Love is there whether you want it or not," Phyllis told me recently. I know that I love Phyllis. She has offered herself as a role model and has inspired me to continue my spiritual journey as a proud woman, to stand as erect as the *vav*, because that is the only way to truly connect. She encourages me to weave in all my colors, the bold, proud parts and the pale, hidden parts, by bringing them out of the closet, removing any remnant of shame, and laughing at the weaving of life. The beauty of all these pieces creates a collage that strengthens my connection to my G!D and makes me happy. With this perspective I am smiling and wondering what comes next. Who knows, maybe a memoir for my daughters to read the parts I could not tell them in person. Then they can have a different role model for truth-telling that may be a transforming element for their lives.

Blessings of the *Vav*

Everyone wants to feel the power of connection. Thank you, Phyllis, for including yourself in my life and letting me feel the joys of being included in yours.

9:55 AM

Monday, August 25, 2008

FINDING ALLIES AND BUILDING BRIDGES

Grand Canyon, 1993

I have been trying to seek out other voices that would support *Agudat HaVav*, the Society of the *Vav*. Each time I notice a universal truth, I feel the walls I set up to keep me safe, coming down. *Yes and* becomes a mantra, as I add another piece of wisdom in another voice/language and I begin to see that all these varied paths have one intention — to heal the world. And I feel less alone and more supported as I walk my path.

I am always reminding myself that life is improvisational, so why not pull from the experts on improv wisdom? I found Avish Parashar on Google and his work supports the universal truth that life is fluid, dynamic, always changing, and always connected to the next, previous, and simultaneous moment.

Susan Scott, author of *Fierce Conversations*, and Marshal Goldsmith, author of *What Got You Here Won't Get You There*, write about the *and* versus the *but*, and how the power of our words indicates our intention. *But* has the power to make one right and another wrong, to negate anything that comes before it. *And* connotes an acceptance of multiple realities where all is real and cannot be rationalized away.

In mediation and when people are coming together to create something that did not exist before, I learned from Comedy Central's Stephen Colbert that it is imperative that each voice be valid. Using *and* or *yes, and* allows the flow of thought without one-upping each other, putting the ego to rest.

Several years ago, Toyota's Scion division created a powerful video advertisement as part of its United by Individuality marketing campaign. The ad begins with various models of cars coming together in the desert, with the tagline: "It is that which makes us different that brings us together." How far I often feel from that moment.

The sages tell us that when the Hebrews gathered around Mt. Sinai to hear the Ten Sayings, to see the sound and hear the light, each person was placed at a specific spot to hear their piece of truth that everyone has a responsibility to fulfill in their lifetime. We are taught not to covet, for each of us has a path that we must stay true to, no matter the distractions we encounter. I am especially aware of my covetous thoughts — when I want to be someone else or do something else — when I am off the path. So I use the thought and emotion as a red flag to come back to center, to be tender to myself, and then begin again by turning, by staying true to me.

Falling asleep is so easy, it is an automatic reflex and easier than staying awake and making my life matter. Settling means staying in line and living a vanilla life. I want more: Frida Kahlo is my hero because, as an artist, she expressed herself through her art with a great flare. So is Cher, who is constantly reinventing herself. I can live without the surgery, even though sometimes I wonder how I got these wrinkles when I am feeling so young and alive! Another paradoxical moment of *and*.

Blessings of the *Vav*

And the beat goes on and on and on and on....

7:36 AM

Thursday, September 4, 2008

LEARNING TO BE HELD IN ELUL

Sculpture in Brookgreen Gardens, Myrtle Beach, SC

Elul, the last month of the Hebrew wisdom calendar, is an opportunity for transformation, for returning to my true self. In *Kabbalah Month by Month*, Mindy Ribner writes that it is a time to complete unfinished business, plan for the future, and deepen a relationship with G!D — and to do all this with kindness.

Blessings of Mindfulness and Being Awake

When Holly was nine she asked her mom, one of my best friends, if I was gay. Her mother replied, "Why don't you ask her yourself?" and Holly responded, "I do not want to hurt her feelings."

What is it that this wise, curious, sensitive nine-year-old already knew?

Another daughter of a dear friend, Kendall — who was in college and in the process of coming-out as lesbian — asked me, "What would you do if your daughter told you she was gay?" I replied, "I would be concerned because it would be a very hard life."

Kendall went away angry, sad, and confused. She both valued the truth and wanted to prove me wrong.

When I remember these events and my heart has closed to the part of me that loves women, I ask myself, "What would I be without the thought that being lesbian is something I have to be careful with, like a sharp knife or lit match?"

And when I withhold the fact that I love women, I ask myself, "What kind of emotional damage do I think I am protecting others from? And do I not think leaves a legacy of fear of being one's self with my daughters and their offspring?"

In the several years that I have lived a life of loving women, I have had many opportunities to see the joys and gifts of being a lesbian woman. There were also situations where I reached out to someone I thought might be lesbian or gay to offer a helping hand, and have been told to mind my own business — or that I was incorrect!! Gay-dar gone wrong!

How long does it take to learn that who you are is someone not many want to be?

In my doctoral dissertation, which explored the coming-out process for lesbian women, I wrote that the definition of lesbian is "affectional and/or sexual relationships with women." When I tell this to women cousins and friends, some say, "Not me!" and others say, "Well, I guess I am lesbian." I can accept both responses, and I feel a lot safer around women who admit that their love of women is so amazing and valid that they can give themselves an adjective that others might find repulsive.

And: Building a World of Connection through Jewish Mystical Wisdom

I often wonder how long it will take to love my many colors, and to make that a priority over others' abhorrence.

When I travel by air my daughter, Ilana, often blesses me that I should sit next to an angel. Yesterday my angel was a man who lives in the same town as my daughter Andrea, and is a distant relative of her husband. A delightful flying partner, he shared his life story and engaged with mine. I try to be aware of my stereotypes and yet am sometimes unconsciously incompetent. There was something about the way my angel moved, his language and quick wit, that made me think he was a gay man. And I was hoping for a real conversation.

As the plane got closer to our destination, I struggled for what seemed like forever about how to approach the subject delicately. I knew there were some gay men in my son-in-law's family and I was hoping my angel was one of them. I cautiously asked if he had heard of Soulforce or Mel White, one of its founders. "Sounds familiar," this polite Southerner responded, and then he asked what they were. I took a very deep breath, prayed for Divine intervention, and said Mel White is the co-founder of a nonviolent Christian organization that supports gays and lesbians. Without a beat, he said his brother is gay, lives in San Francisco with his partner, and is active in Human Rights Campaign.

I relaxed, having passed through the first gate, and felt both relieved and disappointed as we continued to engage in conversations about family and gay issues. Then he told me he had divorced after 21 years of marriage to a wonderful woman, and that many of his friends thought he was gay. He did not think so. I told him about my research on coming-out and that others often know before we do. He said he understood that one, having recently decided to run for political office; when he told his friends, they responded, "At last!" and "Great!"

Then I made my boldest move and said I had brought up the gay issue because I thought that perhaps he was gay. He laughed and said, "Not right now," and that he would think on it. I said his knowing would come from his heart, and he agreed. I told him the Holly story, and he said he understood, because some of his family members had to work at accepting his brother.

As the plane landed and we walked off in different directions, I watched as he headed toward his gate and thought, "What a lovely sashay."

What happens when you dare to tell the truth and stand in awe and delight at being received?

After all these years of loving women and men, counseling lesbians and gay men, conducting workshops on making the professional environment gay-friendly, and encouraging people to come-out, maybe I am beginning to own the thought that being different is not dangerous. That perhaps being *out* can bring me closer *in* to relationships.

Maybe I can act on the fact that in accepting my differentness I can also become more consciously competent in accepting others' uniqueness. Oh, dear, what will I be when those judging thoughts only choke me for a little bit of time? LOL — laughing out loud — my grandsons would say!

Blessings of the *Vav*

Saying *yes, and* to life is following the Hebrew wisdom of *choose life* and trusting that there is something bigger than me making the world a better place. I have only to love and be me, be authentic, and not try to save the world as I already am. Hebrew wisdom also teaches that in saving one life you have saved the world!!! *Halleluya!!*

2:00 PM

Sunday, September 28, 2008

Shalom:
Saying Goodbye
and Hello

Old Sheldon Church Ruins, Yemassee, SC

Tomorrow night as the sun sets I will join Jews all over the world in honoring the ending of the year 5768, celebrating the birth of the world, and welcoming the new year, 5769. I am so excited and ready. There has been much intensity in this last month of creativity and travel; I am ready to pause and notice the moment and be with my people.

It is a time of renewal, of coming back to my true self, forgiving myself and others, and opening of the Book of Life. We will chant on Rosh Hashana and Yom Kippur, "And who will die and who will live?" I take a deep breath as I think about these words; they remind me how much I do not know, how much I can influence, and how much I have to learn.

Letting go of the past and making room for the next moment is a dance I am learning. Sometimes I am awkward in learning the dance steps and sometimes I have to repeat over and over again, like the character in *Groundhog Day*. I am laughing at myself, knowing that I am not laughing alone.

5768 has been an extraordinary year of letting go and uncovering my heart. This blog has been a vessel for shedding *klipot*, the covering of my heart and soul, so I can be more authentic with myself and others, and do my part in healing the world. This week's Torah portion makes clear that G!D is aware of the concealed places and is the uncoverer of the heart. So as I do my striptease dance, She is right there catching the veils and smiling at my courage to be me after all these years. I am amazed that I have not given up, even when I wanted to.

So the circle of life continues; it is a circle to me, a spiral continuing to move outward and upward, embracing more and more love with each cycle, each threshold I cross over.

Blessings of the *Vav*

Life is a cycle of hellos and goodbyes, on and on through eternity, so why not join in choosing life, since I have a partner at each crossing.

3:28 PM

Friday, November 7, 2008

RESIDUALS OF A LIFE OUT OF CONTROL

Beach refuse, Sullivan's Island, SC

Today I missed a client's appointment. My responsible, respectful, kind adult was not in control and my little girl focused only on wanting to play. So after coming home from a shopping spree I hunted down a good movie and drove 30 minutes to a place I had never been to before. I was determined to be spontaneously frivolous.

"Oh, my G!D, what have I done?" I shuddered when I checked my phone and discovered I had missed the appointment, and was reminded of the time I had bounced a check to my therapist. I had sat in a pool of shame, a dysfunctional patient and graduate student, and my therapist laughed and told me about the time she had bounced a check and realized her life was out of control.

Blessings of the *Vav*

Sometimes holding all of life's realities is like attempting to juggle everyone else's needs and not including myself. And all I can do is laugh, learn, forgive, apologize, and move on! And thank G!D for Shabbas, a moment to regroup and listen deeply to the me who felt dissed, and offer a gratis session to my client! *Halleluya!!!!!*

⌨ **6:47 AM**

Friday, November 7, 2008

Prayer to a Compassionate G!d

Geranium

Yesterday I listened to a radio show in which people were talking about the power of prayer that helped them pass the amendment that would not only limit my rights and those of other lesbian and gay people in Florida and California, but the rights of many people who choose to live together and not marry. I wonder, "Who is their God who takes sides to discriminate against me?" I have a friend whose body is filled with cancerous tumors and we are beginning a prayer circle for her through the Internet. I believe in praying for healing that is about self-love. What is so different about this kind of prayer? I am asking for something that does not exclude someone else's human rights.

I am asking myself why I did not consider praying that the Florida amendment would not pass. Why did I think it was only necessary to pass out information, write letters, send money, and talk to people? What kept me from asking my G!D to help me have the strength and courage to love and accept myself, in contrast to the hatred of gays and lesbians in the world?

I learned from a rabbi that we tend to be logicians who stay in our heads, forgetting we live in all four worlds: physical, intellectual, emotional, and spiritual. I needed to remember that my G!D is a G!D of compassion and I can set a *kavana*, an intention, that is nonlinear and inclusive and does not take sides. I know I am held in G!D's womb, the Compassionate One, and like the twins Esau and Jacob, I can continue to wrestle and come out alive.

Hebrew wisdom teaches that prayer comes from the heart. The wisdom of my heart knows this amendment to the Florida constitution is discriminatory and limiting. I wonder what kept me from going deeply inside, setting a *kavana* for the highest good for both sides, and talking with my G!D? And then listening to the voice of *chesed* and *gevura*, lovingkindness and strength, that blend with the energy of the heart, *tiferet*, beauty and equanimity.

So I set an intention to have more conversations with my G!D, in and out of prayer.

Blessings of the *Vav*

Sometimes I have to hold my passion, my logical thinking, and my relationship with my G!D together. Questioning and wrestling with my G!D and then listening deeply may help me heal as the covering of my heart slowly melts away, and for a moment I will feel a part of the world I often protect myself from.

📻 *10:39 AM*

Monday, November 17, 2008

Getting the Word Out

We Need Each Other

How does an introvert express the deep desires of her heart without preaching or pushing her values and views on others? I started making specialized business cards.

Several years ago I was obsessed with asking people to pray for peace in the Middle East. On one side of the business cards I printed, "Take three minutes to pray for peace in the Middle East." On the other side I typed the words of a song by Debbie Friedman based on Zacharia's prophetic words: "Not by power and not by might, but by spirit alone shall we all live in peace."

Recently I was obsessed with the phrase, "Love yourself as if you were your own lover." So put that on one side of a business card and on the other, "Why not, you are amazing!" And I passed them out, left them in bathrooms and on shelves where I thought they would be found.

Now I have made postcards to reflect my latest obsession to de-*but* the world through the Hebrew wisdom of the *vav*. One side of the card asks: "Are you a *Vav-nik*?" and explains that, "A *Vav-nik* is one who honors Hebrew wisdom and the linking energy-intelligence of the *vav* through behavior and intent. *Vav*, the sixth letter of the Hebrew alphabet, is most often translated as *and*."

On the other side is written:

Vav-nik Intentions
- We can hold multiple realities and truths
- Life is improvisational and one must learn to dance with the need of the moment, building bridges between people and thoughts
- Our individuality is the gift we bring into collaborating

Vav-nik Behaviors
- Choosing to use the word *and* instead of *but*
- Being able to sit next to an "enemy" and engage in authentic nonjudgmental conversation

Sarah Bernhardt once said to get people to know who you are you must use all modes of connection. In addition to her movie and theater presence, her name was on soaps, food, paper, clothes, and more than I can remember. Now her name is familiar to my generation and other movie buffs.

Perhaps by putting all this energy into honoring the linking energy of the *vav*, it too will become familiar, something people will think about. Perhaps it will set the intention that we are all connected, so we will treat each other with the love we are taught to give to ourselves, to love the stranger as yourself.

Blessings of the *Vav*

There is no end to the realities and the love I can hold and the ways they can be expressed. I am complete, and the story dynamically continues! TG!!!!

⌨ **7:22 AM**

Thursday, November 27, 2008

Challenges of Holding Multiple Realities

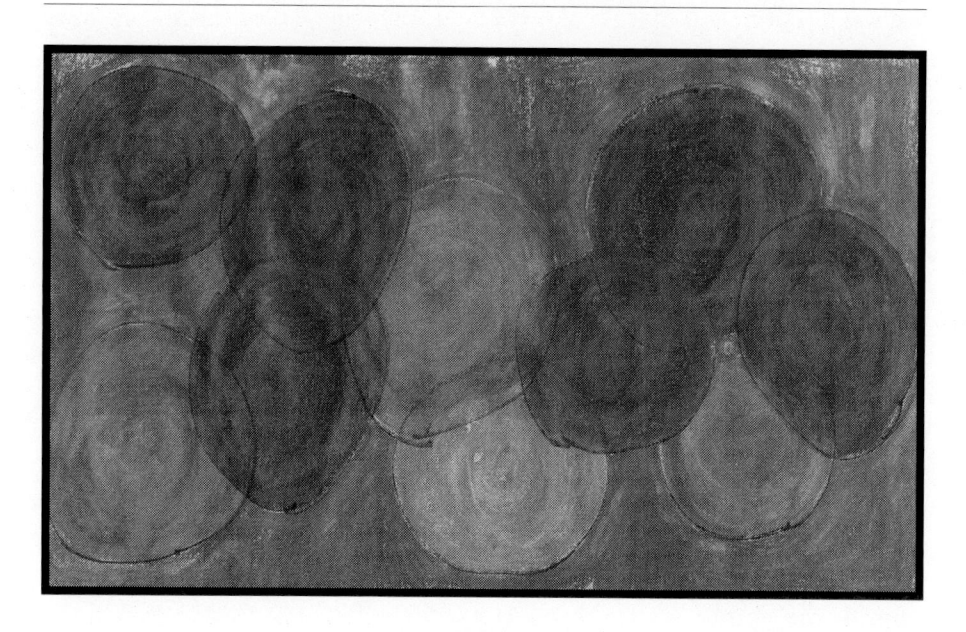

Red Balls

Blessings of Staying Awake

Years ago I went to several workshops on the exploration of the Enneagram, a model of human personality based on nine interconnected personality types. I learned I was a four, which meant I was in the caring group and had a strong need to be different. I felt comfortable with that type. Recently I took an online questionnaire based on the Enneagram and I still came out a four. I was relieved at the consistency and I began thinking of the blessings and curses of uniqueness. My need to be unique often isolates me, keeps me righteous and judging, and gives me a flare if I dare to let my true colors fly.

This Thanksgiving morning, as I lay on the grass overlooking the Intracoastal Waterway, stretching my mind and body in various Pilates poses, a thought crossed my mind: The uniqueness that I hold onto for dear life is everyone's gift from the Divine. And then I asked myself why I was trying so hard to value it as better. I laughed at my inner child screaming, "Mine!" and not wanting to share. And as I heard the yoga teacher telling us that each breath is unique, not to compete with others or myself, I realized how universally true that is.

My thoughts took me down the path that, in Hebrew, the root of the words *breath and soul* are the same, and I was caught up in this Divine, mysterious connection. I told myself that because my soul is unique, with a specific mission, competing or isolating myself only makes my mission more difficult. I began welling up with emotion as we were told to lay in the corpse pose, and then the teacher read Melody Beattie's words on self-love: Love yourself just as you are: Stop coping with events by devaluing yourself. Instead, respond to life by loving and taking care of yourself.

Spiritual Challenge

My life is not separate scenes disconnected from each other. Each scene is vibrantly connected to another and I am connected to them in the same way. To remember what I teach as a rabbi and holder of a universal truth: that it is all about relationships — to space, things, people, weather, souls — and remember that I truly am never alone.

Spiritual Practice

To continue making time during the day to stop, breathe, and focus on the moment, for no other reason than it is my discipline for getting what I want: a deeper relationship with my Divine self that is interrelated with the world.

Blessings of the *Vav*
I am complete and the story dynamically continues! TG!!!!

⌨ *11:16 AM*

Monday, December 22, 2008

MUSING ON THE MOMENT

Multiple Vavs

Blessings of Staying Awake

As I prepared to open my home to celebrate creating my very new real home and the lighting of the first Chanuka lights, I took a moment to write these notes:

Dear Ones,
At this point in time of the longest day, the Winter Solstice, and the shortest night, as we move into the 25th of Kislev, the first night of Chanuka, and a celebration-dedication of my living space, by raising the sides of my tent and welcoming the souls who have soothed my transitional move, I think of you in other physical places and held tenderly here in my heart.

My blessings go to you of peace of mind and heart
Of joy and befriending of the moment
Of friendship and a deep, full breath
To ease adjustments to whatever 2009 will bring.

And may each word of the blessings we say strengthen us
Open our eyes to the beauty around us
And to the abundance of what we have
And may we each feel the Love available any time.

Happy Chanuka, Joyous Solstice, Happy Kwanza, and Merry Merry Christmas!
TZiPi

Spiritual Challenge

To keep my heart open so I can continue to write from it and receive the love that comes back. Also to have the patience with myself and others when I am thrown a curveball and my knees are not as loose as I would like and I trip on my own expectations. Oh, being human is tough sometimes! I am feeling drained from having so many people in my space and being the host, which I love, and I also love my quietude. Taking a hot bath would be great, instead of answering emails, washing the floor, and returning everything I borrowed.

Spiritual Practice

To stop, breathe deeply, smile with happy eyes, and laugh at me. I am in such a habit of judging me when I do not live up to my own expectations. I have to remember to notice and remember I am fluid, not a stone!!!!!

Blessings of the *Vav*
I am complete and the story dynamically continues! TG!!!!

⌨ **3:45 PM**

Friday, December 26, 2008

MEDITATION IS SAVING MY LIFE

Shivering Heart

This post was originally written as if mediation had saved my life and now I was onto other things. The truth is that meditation was the first step toward learning to live with me and the world and my evolving mindfulness practice, where I am being kind to myself, opposing the mind that loves to doubt, judge, numb, and suffer. I have changed the title of this essay to reflect an ongoing meditation practice, so please take that into consideration as you read. Thank you.

Blessings of Being Awake

So again I am giving attention to the fractals in my life, and oh, how I love patterns that repeat themselves. Within them order reigns and I feel held. And each part of a fractal is not the same, they just fall together in love.

I am talking with several of my coaching clients more regularly of the importance of having a spiritual practice. I often use myself as a model, and when I tell them how my meditation practice developed into a mindfulness practice, I often say it saved my life. And I believe it did.

In September of 1996 I arrived on the island of Koh Pang Ghan in the south of Thailand, right before the rainy season. On my way to the Buddhist monastery Wat Kow Tahm for 10 days of silence, I hired a young man to carry me up the mountain on his motor scooter.

Rosemary and Steven Wiseman, my Vipassana instructors, were the best teachers I ever had. They did everything in their power to make it emotionally safe to just *be*. They provided an order of the day with written instructions available on the dining room bulletin board, followed through with what they said they would do, had our personal schedules displayed at a certain time, and modeled their simple teachings. Those 10 days were full of learnings and experiences I value to this day, and I say a deep thank you!

Spiritual Challenge

My new teachers know about the mind that loves to wander, even race, from thought to thought, emotion to emotion. They know the mind loves to suffer. They know we are here to make the world a better place. I knew the first two were true; I had lived what they spoke of, and I was grateful to have lived so long as to learn I am not alone. From my Hebrew wisdom teaching I understand about making the world a better place — *tikun olam*, healing the world — and with self-love I am learning I can be a part of making a difference.

Now, with an opening heart carefully being circumcised, I can appreciate the universal truths of Hebrew wisdom that keep me mindful of the moment and help me learn to live with myself in peace, *shalom*, and as whole, *shalem*. Distractions come like fractals, challenging me to stay true to myself and my values, that all we need is love... da da da da da. I remember a long time ago balking at some young women students who told me they loved me. What do they know of love? I thought to myself while being graciously polite. Now I believe that more and more each day.

Spiritual Practice

To believe and act on the truth that the body is my holy friend, the Indwelling Presence of the Divine. From paying attention to Her I learn what to eat, when to sleep, when to stay away from something, and when to do more! And I have so much still to learn, I am just a beginner.

Every day at the monastery and for at least two years, when I said the following words as a mantra the mind eventually settled down and the heart opened to possibilities:

May I have great compassion for myself as I notice and then let go of the fear, anger, worry, doubt, and ignorance, may I preserve my well being.

May I continue to have the patience, courage, wisdom, and faith to face the problems and challenges that come my way, may I have peace of mind.

My spiritual practice is evolving with prayer, solitude, creativity, and building deeper relationships with my G!D, myself, and others in my life; the many pieces and multiple realities of an improvisational life. I am a *Vav-nik* — of course, what else could be true? I read William P. Young's *The Shack* a few weeks ago and was surprised at how it helped deepen my G!D link. When in tight places I call out, "*Ma yakar hasedecha*, how precious is your lovingkindness," or recite in Hebrew the 13 attributes of G!D, and find myself back in relationship with Her and me, at least until the next distraction.

Blessings of the *Vav*

I am complete and the story dynamically continues! TG!!!!

12:03 PM

Tuesday, December 30, 2008

THERE IS NOTHING SORRY ABOUT YOU

All Roads Lead to Love

Blessings of Being Awake

Lately, I hear the word *sorry* very often. "I am sorry I shut the door in your face" or "I am so sorry about your mother's death" or "So sorry, I did not mean to hurt you" or "I am so sorry I forgot to call and say thank you for the gift." People are trying to be kind and regretful of the behavior that causes others' unhappiness, and in saying "I'm sorry" they are not saying what they really mean. "I'm sorry" is used in place of, "Wow, I wasn't watching the door" or "You must be experiencing so many emotions at your mother's death" or "My intention was not to hurt you" or "Oops, that was unkind of me to not let you know I received your gift."

Spiritual Challenge

When someone says those words to me I have been responding, "There is nothing sorry about you." If they are paying attention, they usually smile and agree with me. I do not want to be right; I want to remind others and myself to live up to our bigness. I am trying to go beyond my disappointment, anger, and frustration when I sent our holiday gift checks and heard nothing! I had to dig deep this time to care for myself, look at what I have, and consciously choose Jerry and Esther Hicks's downstream thinking! Saying *thank you* to those who bring me to the untruth thoughts of separation and isolation takes a lot of inner work. Since I have chosen to love me, I am working hard to take deep breaths and think in *ands* and paradoxes.

Spiritual Practice

Knowing there is nothing sorry about me, I have chosen peace of mind over being stuck in narrow places and being a slave to my thoughts. I have chosen to act in truth and love, as if the amazing people in my life are interrelated with me, and to reach out to them. I decided that when I do not hear from them, I will no longer linger or wonder or wait. So I texted them to find out if they received the gifts. And what gifts I received; more than I ever expected, a continued and deepened relationship! Another gift from You, thank us for staying in touch!

Blessings of the *Vav*

I am complete and the story dynamically continues! TG!!!!

3:06 PM

2009

Thursday, February 12, 2009

Claiming the Liminal Space of Not Knowing

Various kinds of mint tea, Israel

Blessings of Being Awake

My new friend, Eva, told me with a big grin that she is waiting for a new blog entry. I am aware that I have not written anything since December. I am not sure exactly why and I am choosing not to spend time wondering. It is a fact that I am sitting in nothing-viscerally-provoking-me-to-write mode. And spending time in *why?* and *how come?* gets me into a judging place that does not provoke creativity. I am still learning how to inquire with innocent curiosity. So I start from this moment and ask myself, as G!D asked Adam, "*Ayecha*, where are you?" And Adam went into this great storytelling of shame and blame.

I could have looked at my calendar and seen what I have been doing for the past six weeks and explained away my absence from what I am committed to — my writing. In this moment I will not go backward, only notice that I am glad I am making time to write today. I am grateful that I have a computer that is working, and I am well. There is no blame or shame to be fed; only remembering what I love to do and doing it!

Yet maybe I do not know all that I love, and I need to try something different: to try just being instead of doing. I have heard Eboo Patel, founder of the InterFaith Youth Corp, say that leaders do not make excuses — they ask to solve the problem. I often suggest to my clients that contemplation, just being, is a necessary form of strategic planning.

Spiritual Challenge

Not only am I learning to love me, but *how* to love me. Staying focused with my deepest desire for peace of mind, being loving toward myself as my G!D is, and doing what I love is getting easier. To notice that simply *being* is an option and a challenge to the mind, which always wants to be active and changing. I want to learn to be in the liminal space of not knowing. I want to learn to live with ambiguity. I am on a threshold, and I need to limit the wondering and allow life to evolve. The moon is waning, and I need not start any new projects. Social Security just called and I will be getting my benefits beginning in May, so my bills will be paid. I need to be loving to myself, and to try just being and not doing. Writing will wait.

Spiritual Practice

Being in a contemplative state, sitting with myself in kindness, breathing deeply, and getting to know the liminal space of not knowing. In August 1995

I was in that space when I heard, "You are going for a trip around the world." I am a traveler, and perhaps remembering my interpretation of Hebrew wisdom's prayer for all travelers — which eases the moving over thresholds and into transitions — may be helpful. So I started to chant the words whenever the desire for form or permanence arises. Listen, TZiPi, You and the Divine Mystery of All Life are One. You are not alone in this space. *Shma*, listen to your heart's wisdom; you are not separate, dear one, and you are holy as She is holy. Just be and do what you love; sit and have a cup of mint tea and look at the clouds floating through your window.

Blessings of the *Vav*

I am complete and the story dynamically continues! TG!!!!

⌨ **9:07 AM**

Saturday, March 7, 2009

I Feel Known, and You Can't Get Better than That

Flower

Blessings of Being Awake

I have heard my sister-friend, Tziporah, say with her passionate, heavy Brooklyn accent, "He got me." I could feel her heart softening into joy and delight, and my heart joined my friend's. As she spoke I could not remember an experience of being gotten that would have stopped me in my tracks so that I, too, would have spontaneously said out loud, "She got me!" Andrea once spontaneously told me, "I want to be known," and I heard this deep, intuitive response from my very private, introverted daughter. I wanted this for her, and yet was not quite sure what that would look like for me.

Spiritual Challenge

Being known or being gotten requires me to show up, be bold with my energy and light; to be my Self, a leader among leaders, a priest among priests. In his *Book of Letters*, Rabbi Lawrence Kushner writes that the letter vav stands erect in its uniqueness, confident in being separate among others and linking with others to create a whole unity. I am learning that only when I am willing to risk being seen do I have more chances of being gotten and known.

For the past nine years or so, on Friday afternoon I have tried to connect with my daughters, fill them in on my life, ask what is happening in theirs, and bless them with a *Shabbat shalom*, a Sabbath of peace and wholeness. Yesterday Andrea called me and was most energetic as she told me about Oprah's guest, Dustin Lance Black, Academy Award winner for the screenplay written for the movie *Milk*. She explained that her excitement was twofold: first, she was deeply moved by both Dustin's and Harvey Milk's stories; and second, the movie *Milk* had not come to Beaufort and she was frustrated about the kinds of films that came and the duration of their stay. "I will get to see it, yet," she said with great determination.

In her initiating this call I felt deeply connected to my daughter. She was in a tender place of needing to be known, and as I recall the conversation I am noticing the emotions as tears well and fall on my cheeks. And in that moment I smiled; I had been gotten by my first daughter, my friend who was committed to loving and knowing me and my difference, and all within her very homophobic world. For the first time that I can remember, she was the one who brought up this important place for me. I was able to take her knowing me into my body and rejoice in being gotten by her.

Spiritual Practice

In biblical Hebrew the word *known* translates to a sexual experience, as in, "Adam knew Eve." As I heard with Andrea — and saw in the movie *Lost in Translation*, when the main characters enjoy each other in a long-into-the-night, collaborative conversation — an erotic, fully alive moment can happen without sex. Coming-out or self-disclosing can be as easy as getting dressed in your favorite clothes or as hard as stating an opposing opinion to a new friend. My practice is to notice when I withhold me from coming-out, and to love that frightened part. So I have begun taking voice lessons and playing with coming-out from my whole body, in all kinds of new ways, in a safe place. And maybe get to know me and get myself in whole new ways!

12:58 PM

Saturday, March 7, 2009

I Am Reb Tzipi and I Am Here to Recruit You

Collage from handmade paper, Sri Aurobindo Ashram, India

Blessings of Being Awake

As I cut out the phrase "I got milk" from the magazine ad, I felt I had shifted to thinking instead of intuiting. The theme at the collage workshop was, "Who am I in this moment?" and I was compelled to place the phrase on my project, and not to give up on my intuition. The word *milk* reminded me of the late Harvey Milk — the gay political activist who had become one of my heroes — and the powerful phrase he used to begin his speeches, "I'm Harvey Milk and I'm here to recruit you."

Spiritual Challenge

I was driving my aunts to the airport and as we drove by a sign I read it out loud. Aunt Estelle, sitting in the passenger seat, said, "What did you say?" I laughed and repeated the words, then said I have the Abrams trait of reading signs out loud. We all laughed — Aunt Estelle does the same thing — and Aunt Frannie said, "You don't have Abrams traits, you have your dad's warm and friendly, *we need each other attitude*." She was right, even if I do not like admitting how much I am like my dad. My responsibility and challenge is to honor that trait and make it mine. I do stand on his shoulders. As a Jew I know how life-affirming it is to have allies, and holding the intention that we need each other helps in walking the path of Oneness, rather than separation, which is so psychically painful. Moving beyond the doubting mind and trusting in people's goodness is a challenge for me as I get close to others.

Spiritual Practice

"I am a *Vav-nik* and am living an inclusive life," I say into the mirror. I continue, "Hi, I am Rabbi TZiPi Radonsky and I am here to recruit you to be a *Vav-nik*, to stand up tall and be the leader you were born to be." I thought about my ancestor, Sarah, and wondered if she ever said, "Hi, Hebrews, I am Sarah and I am here to recruit you to believe in the One Unknowable God." Someone recently said they never heard of a *Vav-nik* and yet had heard of a *Lamed Vavnik*. I quickly responded, "Being a *Vav-nik* is the first step in becoming a *Lamed Vavnik*." A *Lamed Vavnik* in mystical Hebrew wisdom is one of the 36 righteous people alive in the world at any given time. They are ordinary people who humbly hold the mystical key to mending the world.

Hi, sister and brother leader, I am Reb TZiPi and I am here to recruit you. I am on a mission to make the world a better place through de-*butting* the world and I am asking for your support. **6:53 PM**

Thursday, March 19, 2009

Letting Myself Back into My Heart

"Row, row, row your boat, gently down the stream...."

Blessings of Being Awake

I did not know I had let myself out of my heart and then I read the thought for today, "I forgive myself for not doing all I had I promised myself because I did not feel good enuf." As soon as I read it I knew I had been journeying away from me, my G!D, and my heart. I could feel the visceral movement through the layers of protection I surround my heart with.

Spiritual Challenge

Today something woke me up and I am noticing something is missing and I am out of alignment. The website is launched and I am scared; can I follow through? I am more visible, out there in my eyes, and the old fears around being safe and doing it "right" arise. Can I notice these thoughts and keep believing in me, even when I am sitting in not knowing? When trying to lead the community out of slavery, Moses tells Pharaoh, "We will not know how we are to serve G!D until we arrive there." I am a lifelong learner of how to love me in each moment, and it is fun doing this exploring.

Spiritual Practice

I can still hear Stephen Levine's voice at the workshop I attended in the early 1990s in Chapel Hill, "Let yourself back into your heart," and I remember the visceral response to doing as I was directed. I can do this each moment; a simple breath, a thought, and I am here, no longer the wandering Jew. I am back in my heart with my G!D and me. In this moment I am smiling and laughing, opening my mouth, relaxing all the muscles of my face, being young at heart, body, and mind! "Home!" I say to myself as tears well and my heart sings, "Row, row, row my boat gently down the stream, merrily, merrily, merrily, merrily, life is but a dream!"

Blessings of the *Vav*

I am complete and the story dynamically continues! TG!!!!

8:00 AM

Saturday, April 25, 2009

"And" Expands My Heart and My Perspective

Shy Flower

Blessings of Being Awake

Recently I have noticed that the anger I had been harboring toward my father since he died has slowly been receding. I even said something nice about him the other day. I was surprised, and then it happened again — later that week I spontaneously quoted his favorite phrase, "We need each other." I was puzzled; I thought I had left his legacy off my agenda when I decided that I was not going to stand on his shoulders. I began to notice the tightness in my chest soften when I thought of him and of his G!D. This emotional shift seems to have brought a different perspective.

Spiritual Challenge

I need to set an intention to remember that everything changes and to notice that there is always something I am not seeing. If I open my eyes, perhaps I can see what on first glance is hidden. I want to believe that neither the joy nor the pain is forever. If I do not harbor the pain and make myself a victim or a hero to my emotions and thoughts, this too will pass; I can and will let go of what is no longer useful to the nurturing of my soul. That is what Harville Hendrix teaches in *Keeping the Love You Find*: A healing happens when you stick in relationships long enough to heal those childhood wounds, even with the dead.

Spiritual Practice

The other day I suggested to a client that she might want to try the phrase, "I know nothing." She did not like this, so I added the other half of the truth, "I am a very smart woman and I know nothing." She liked the blending of these two truths. Since this conversation I have found myself laughing and saying that phrase, opening my heart and being curious. Moving beyond the narrow place — which we call Mitzrayim, the Egypt of our slavery — and gaining perspective is like sitting in meditation, not moving, just allowing the sounds, sensations, feelings, thoughts to be noticed. I give myself the option of keeping them around or letting them go and noticing what arises next. I need lots of practice off the cushion to do this. Sometimes I can do it for my clients better than I can do it for me.

So I will continue to attempt to do for me what I do for them — not to be a slave to thoughts or emotions that distract me from being kind and loving to me, the core teaching of Hebrew wisdom. It is all about love. These seven weeks between Passover and Shavuot are opportunities to refine my soul to prepare for receiving our holy teachings. Using the priestly letter vav that connects heaven and earth in my life as a tool to gain perspective is my pilgrimage home.

Blessings of the *Vav*

I am complete and the story dynamically continues! TG!!!!

7:54 AM

Saturday, April 25, 2009

Transparency and Telling the Truth

Reflection of limbs over water, Aiken, SC

Blessings of Being Awake

I love hearing the word *transparency*. My visceral response to experiencing the directness of stating the facts is to light up inside and feel clean, like a shiny, squeaky-clean baby's bottom! I am aware that what I know and do not speak out loud gets in the way of what I do say! Often I wish I were a child again, with no inhibitions — or like my father was at the end of his life: Just say it like it is, TZiPi! Several TV interviews and some collaborative meetings lately have been like this for me, and I revel in those moments of speaking from my heart. And I want more!

Spiritual Challenge

Transparency demands a lot of me. I have to acknowledge my emotions in the moment and then step through the barriers they may create to the other side — truth in that moment. In *The Managerial Moment of Truth*, Fritz and Bodaken call it MMOT, and write that it can improve performance and increase productivity. As I step forward into the unknown I am deepening a relationship with myself. Only through this disclosing am I acknowledging what is, clearing the air, and creating a frame of connection so we each are building a relationship of mutual pleasures. My behavior is reflecting my belief that what I say is important in that moment. I do not have to hide the conversation in some corner or wait for the perfect moment.

The other night I was with a large group of people celebrating a birthday, and across the table I saw some friends who I wanted to ask about a ride to the airport. I hesitated and then gave myself permission to not wait another moment. I felt awkward talking in public about a private thing, and as I spoke the world did not fall apart. So I walked across the room and began the conversation with Joel about a ride to the airport. And he told me about his mom and his concerns about her health. The conversation and exchange left me feeling free and unencumbered. It made me wonder about waiting to tell someone you love her, and how many sad stories I have heard about missing the moment.

Spiritual Practice

I will set an intention to notice what I value and try to be consistent in integrity with myself. To stay awake to what I believe and just live it! Oy vey! What discipline this requires — "to do my best," as Miguel Ruiz reminds me in *The Four Agreements*. As the teachings of Hebrew wisdom inform my life, discipline brings me closer to the Divine and to the truth that we are all One heart beating. Isn't that what we all want? To not feel alone, to be able to cut through the crap or the unsaid and get to the core of the issue. Unpeeling the layers is an art that takes lots of practice. Keeping my mouth open and breathing deeply assists in breaking an old pattern of silence. I once kept my mouth shut for fear of reprisal, avoiding the truth and the consequences it would bring to an already dysfunctional system.

The truth is I am learning that I can take care of myself. I am following my voice coach's teaching to relax the muscles of my face, to allow the smile to emerge and reflect the joy in my heart. To continue to be aware of what keeps me silent and what I experience when I let the words spring from this heart. I set an intention to speak as readily as I purchase a gift for my daughters, giving it to them immediately instead of waiting for a birthday, Chanuka, or the next time I see them. Hebrew wisdom teaches that each moment is a beginning, so I will be a beginner, as the lama in Nepal suggested we all are.

Blessings of the *Vav*

I am complete and the story dynamically continues! TG!!!!

8:14 AM

Tuesday, May 12, 2009

Building on a Legacy While Finding Balance

Close-up of pink flower

Blessings of Being Awake

Sometimes I wish my mind would just stop for a moment — and then it happens, and I wonder if I too have "the disease."

As I was looking through one of several books I have lying open around my home, I read a phrase that sang to me, from *The Blue Sweater* by Jacqueline Novogratz: "Together we can do anything." The visual image is of many bodies working together for a common good, creating high energy. It is the next step after, "We need each other." It is a doing. I have noticed that I like doing, being physically involved in an activity. I love to travel, and yet nothing felt right until my cousin Linda said she and Michael were planning to go canoeing in the south of France in August, and my heart got excited. Now that sounds like fun! And I remember paddling down the river with Tracey and Joan, totally involved, body, mind, and spirit when I visited them in North Carolina.

Spiritual Challenge

I remember once taking part in a road trip with many cars following the same route. I felt the electricity and excitement. I seek that high in between the quiet times of being alone, musing, and working independently — well, just my G!D and me. The challenge is remembering that *together* does not have to mean lots of people. Recently I watched a TED lecture in which Elizabeth Gilbert talks about the creative process being a collaboration of the Divine and you — that worrying about doing it alone can be daunting and can bring on writers' block, among other narrow, grasshopper-like feelings. When I remember the muse, diva, G!D, however you want to call "it," there is a truth that creates a rippling effect to the autonomic nervous system, causing a deep, full breath.

Spiritual Practice

When I was visiting the Sri Aurobindo Ashram in Pondicherry, India, I met a devotee from Japan who had her paintings on display. When asked about her creative process, she spoke about her inspiration that came from a Divine source. I remember wondering what that feels like, to be inspired by the Divine, and wanting a piece of whatever that was. While living in Gainesville, FL, in the late 1970s, I went to see *For Colored Girls Who Have Considered Suicide / When the Rainbow Is Enuf* by Ntozake Shange. One character said, "I found god in myself and I loved her," and that phrase has stuck with me all these years. While I have practiced and imagined the Indwelling Presence, *Shechina*, within me, not until I read *The Shack* did it actually happen. My practice now is to notice my child spirit, who sometimes is frightened of the night and the bullies, the alone-ness and the inactive, non-doing time, and soothe her with knowing the Divine energy. In these moments I am feeding the hungry ghost; a smile relaxes on my face, and I am resting in the arms of my Beloved.

Blessings of the *Vav*

I am complete and the story dynamically continues! TG!!!!

4:29 AM

Tuesday, May 12, 2009

MEMORIES

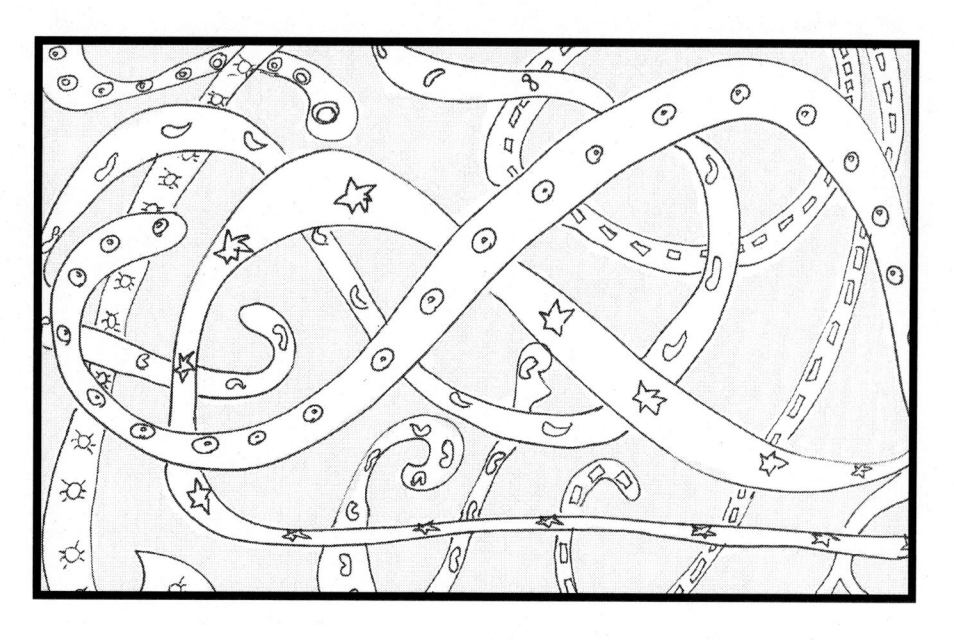

Eternal Travel

Blessings of Being Awake

I was up too early this morning trying to keep control of my schedule, and as I stood in the kitchen, thoughts floated in and out of my consciousness. I remembered that my Uncle Harry (of blessed memory) once told me I was a writer. He was famous to me, and his words and our relationship meant a lot to me. If he were around I would thank him for blessing me. My friend Arthur, who is a publisher and a writer himself, once told me that if you write, you are a writer. I believe that, and yet it does not honor the uniqueness of each of us to offer our perceptions, which fill emptiness, stimulate curiosity, deepen understanding, enhance imagination, inform, entertain, or just keep track of a very busy and full life.

Spiritual Challenge

I want to honor Uncle Harry, the Doc, my dad's oldest brother, by dedicating this writing to him. I cannot tell his widow or his son, because they have disappeared without a trace. I want to reach across time to when we were together near Camelback Mountain in Arizona or on Temple Street in Newton, MA, and laugh and cry with him. He was my hero. He never wrote anything that was published, yet he had many friends who did. He was written about in a book that still sits on my bookshelf, *Don't Push the River* by Barry Stevens. He was also my role model; he was a doctor of the mind who dedicated himself to the well being of his patients. And he and my Aunt Norma always welcomed me into their home. I often smile remembering to honor the truth. I am not alone, even though I am an only child brought up by two fiercely independent parents who taught me to depend on no one. I love dispelling those facts while remembering those souls whose essences are tightly woven into my being-ness. Thank you, Uncle Harry, for caring for me so well!

Spiritual Practice

Write, write, write, I tell my clients. Express yourself on paper, do morning writings, as Julia Cameron suggests in *The Artist's Way* or Natalie Goldberg teaches in *Writing Down the Bones*. Tell your story. Writing grounds me in the moment, makes me stop and do something that connects the dots of my life. While I was away from home space the last two weeks, in my journal each morning I noted the Hebrew and secular calendar day, counted the *omer*, and wrote what I had been doing the previous day and what I was about to do. I let the words, feelings, and thoughts flow onto the page. When I got home I had a record of my journey and while I was gone I never felt lonely, as I was present with me the whole way. What a gift from you, Uncle Harry; thanks for seeing me in a bigger way than I could see me in that moment.

Blessings of the *Vav*

I am complete and the story dynamically continues! TG!!!!

⌨ *6:41 AM*

Sunday, June 14, 2009

Relationships Take Time

Animals and Flora, Camouflage

Blessings of Being Awake

I have had the title for this blog for three weeks, ever since I exchanged my BlackBerry Curve for a BlackBerry Storm. I wanted so much for our relationship to be mutual and I kept working at being patient, breathing deeply, slowing down. Nothing seemed to work. So I decided I had tried enough and I wanted my life to be easier than this! I needed to take action to make it happen.

Spiritual Challenge

I'm working with a client who had been reading one of Eckhart Tolle's books and wanted to focus on getting rid of the ego. I said that before you get rid of the ego, you need to notice when it takes over your life. Saying this, I saw no connection between the topic and me. LOL, as my grandsons would text me. Laugh out loud at me! That BlackBerry Storm was a status symbol for me, and here I thought I was settling into the place of being comfortable with my working-class background! No way! I may be a working-class girl, and I am also upper-middle class in terms of liking to have nice things!

Spiritual Practice

Continue to listen to the patterns in my life that my clients bring me and notice when the teaching is for me, too. And laugh at the joy of learning new things about me! Relationships sometimes have to be transformed out of the foreground of my life, and not be ongoing. I sold my BlackBerry Storm and got another Curve — and this time it is hot pink!

Blessings of the *Vav*

I am complete and the story dynamically continues! TG!!!!

7:19 PM

Sunday, June 14, 2009

BEING

Beach refuse, Sullivan's Island, SC

Blessings of Being Awake

I could have gone drumming today and filled the time with something I enjoy doing. Or I could have stayed at home, played in the garden, rested at my leisure, and enjoyed just being here. The little voice kept saying the class is now and you might have to wait another three weeks to go. I heard it and then said, "Yeah, but I could stay home, read a good book, do some computer work, and take a nap!"

Spiritual Challenge

When do I know which voice to listen to? To my head or my heart. The feelings in the heart said take care of you today; no need to leave, there is plenty to do here. Integrate what you have been doing — study sailing literature, practice singing, oil the leather car upholstery, weed the garden. Just be. Take a nap, put your feet above your head, lie on your back, or just notice your breath.

Spiritual Practice

Slowing down to really live what I teach: to be present for me and pay attention to the emotions, feelings, thoughts, and body sensations. When I know that I am loving me as only I can, I am satisfied beyond words.

Blessings of the *Vav*

I am complete and the story dynamically continues! TG!!!!

7:40 PM

Wednesday, July 8, 2009

MULKA —
MOTHERS UNITED FOR LOVING-KINDNESS & ALLIES

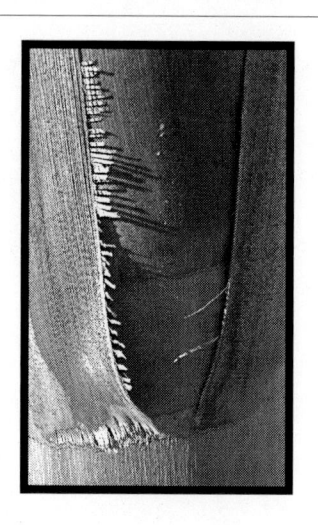

Palm tree trunk

Blessings of Being Awake

I am aware of the disharmony in my body-mind-spirit universe when I am confronted with unkind tones from another. I do not like it, and I cannot figure out how to let the other know. The words given to me feel sharp, dull, and neither my heart nor mind is prepared. I am silent, responding from a place of fear of disconnection. I am in the midst of a monologue that I thought was a dialogue. I know I can do it to others, too. I came home not liking myself after a recent visit with my mother. I was disappointed that I had not kept my promise to myself to be kind to her. I was attempting to break a family pattern, and sometimes I am not capable of pulling it off. Sometimes when I attempt to set boundaries I am awkward, and my language patterns and emotional intelligence are limited. I am feeling stunted.

Spiritual Challenge

To be loving-kind to myself when I do not live up to my own standards of behavior. To laugh out loud, instead of digging in the knife to cut out the bad stuff. To begin to peel off the outer layers of self-doubt and get to the core of my pure soul. And to remember to sing and LOL at, and with, me.

Spiritual Practice

Each day as I awaken and look out at the water and trees, listening to the birds chirping and watching my chest rise and fall with each breath, I will remember that free will and loving-kindness are choices on the list of options, and I can put myself at the top of that list.

MULKA: a virtual reality sponsored by the Society of the *Vav*.

Blessings of the *Vav*

I am complete and the story dynamically continues! TG!!!!

1:41 PM

Wednesday, July 8, 2009

STRATEGIC PLANNING

Wild geese grazing

Blessings of Being Awake

A friend asked me what I thought of Michael Jackson's death. I was surprised, as I had not heard or read anything. In that moment I became aware that I had cut myself off from the world outside my home. Occasionally, I am like these geese, head down, nose to the grindstone, a puritan work ethic taking over my life. Everything here is nurturing me, so why bother to look around?

Spiritual Challenge

A teacher once said if you are going to live a spiritual life you have to read the newspaper and watch TV. Wedemeyer and Jue write that to live a spiritual life means to transcend compartmentalization and have a balance in one's life. I need to pay attention to the signs that it is time to lift my head up and stretch my neck!

Spiritual Practice

To take time regularly to assess the balance of work-play, private-public, doing-being, solo-collaboration. This is all a part of being kind to myself, a *Vav-nik*.

Blessings of the *Vav*

I am complete and the story dynamically continues! TG!!!!

2:15 PM

Friday, July 10, 2009

LIVING THE FUTURE TODAY

Wild iris, Israel

Blessings of Being Awake

I have been writing a lot lately of what my life looks like right now. I am imagining my future and loving the dreams and the sensations that arise, bringing the joy into the moment.

Spiritual Challenge

Do I dare to be the wild thing that feels no self-pity and focuses only on staying on the bough? Am I *G.I. Jane*, up for doing whatever it takes to be where I imagine myself being?

Spiritual Practice

Noticing the fear — the desire to stay in the Goldilocks zone of not too hot and not too cold — and breathing deep as I sail to catch the wind, living my life fully.

Blessings of the *Vav*

I am complete and the story dynamically continues! TG!!!!

⌨ **7:06 AM**

Saturday, July 25, 2009

THE WEEKLY NEW AND GOOD

Spider web

Blessings of Being Awake

Today I brought my 14-year-old grandson, Drew, back to his mom after a fun, athletic, funny, exploring, and bonding week. When I arrived back home the place felt empty and I experienced a feeling of loneliness. As I slid down into the loneliness feeling, the phone rang. Tziporah was calling for our weekly "Shabbat new and good conversation." We had promised each other to meet every Shabbat and share the good stuff that had happened that week. She started by telling me about a few disappointments, and that she was not feeling well. I listened and then asked, "What good happened?" As she spoke, her voice changed and she began to sound energized. She remembered lots of good stuff, including a new client! Then it was my turn and she began with a question, "Did you draw the picture of you with the magic wand?" Wam! She got me by reminding me of where I had left off before Drew came. I had gotten so caught up in being the grandmother who focuses only on pleasing another that I had forgotten the other parts of me!

Spiritual Challenge

In busy times it is so easy to forget me and the promises I make to myself. If I surround myself with people who love me and remind me of my promises to myself, then when I fall back into old habits and familiar pain I will be reminded of my choices. My week with Drew had been fantastic; I felt like a young woman, sailing, snorkeling, and playing tennis with this dynamic and very active young man. And now the vacation was over and he was gone and I felt a loss of him and of me.

Spiritual Practice

Take 10 minutes a day to be with me, meditate, focusing on my choices for gentleness and nonaggression. Keep my journal every day and look back to check for alignment. Laugh a lot, ask for forgiveness of myself when I mess up, and keep placing me back into my heart, where she belongs! Share good things with friends. And share my practice with my guests, including my grandson. Teach by role modeling.

5:51 PM

Friday, September 18, 2009

ENTERING THE
PROMISE LAND

Grand Canyon, 1993

Blessings of Being Awake

When I looked at the date on the last blog entry I could not believe it was so far away. Where have I been? Well, I have been to Prague to visit Phyllis for a week, to Boston for Joni and Stefan's wedding, to Greensboro to work, and a glorious return to India for two weeks of leadership training work. There must be so much to write about.

Spiritual Challenge

Where do I begin? It has been an amazing spiritual journey. In fact from India I signed an email "the spiritual pilgrim." I am waking up to say to myself, "Right place, right time! When are you going to understand that all you have to do is show up?! You are the vessel, you are the wisdom, you are TZiPi, authentic, kind, brilliant, focused, humbly human!"

Spiritual Practice

Noticing the doubt that sneaks in and holding on to the intention of a circumcised heart; keeping the neck loose as I did when I first arrived in India. It was so simple, like I had been doing it all my life, moving my head from right to left! The song that comes from my heart is the refrain, "love is all you need, love is all you need, love is all you need!"

So as 5769 ends and 5770 begins at sundown tonight, I make a promise to myself: I will be the *vav* I was meant to be. I will stand erect, chest open, shoulders back, bracing against my erect, strong back as I move forward into the promised land, into the abundance waiting for me and anyone else who takes the same risks. It is there and I am going after it. I can feel the joy, taste the deliciousness of the fruit, and feel the welcome of all those who meet me. I am home and in joy!!!

Blessings of the *Vav*

There is always one more thing and it does not have to be doom; it can be joy. Why not prophesize from hope, connection, and love, and truly live that truth?

1:01 PM

Sunday, September 20, 2009

Lamed Vavniks

Wood carver, Poland

Blessings of Being Awake

A few weeks ago when I was doing some training in India I gave away my *Vav-nik* cards. In wanting them to understand where the card fits into a larger frame of being leaders, I told this story.

In Hebrew wisdom tradition, at any one time there are 36 righteous people walking the earth. The term *Lamed Vavnik* comes from the number that each Hebrew letter represents: *lamed* is 30 and *vav* is 6, thus *Lamed Vavnik* is 36. These righteous people have a soul whose primary mission is to do the mending of the tears in the fabric of the universe, to heal the separation we experience that does not exist in reality. When the story of the *Lamed Vavnik* was first told to me, he is a tailor who appears to be sewing fabric, yet is going deeper into the soul of the person whose clothes he is repairing.

Our host in India, Anupam, smiled as he heard the story. When I finished he said he liked how I had explained about the righteous people. In that moment I was aware that I had reached across cultures and found common ground.

Spiritual Challenges

When I heard Rabbi Dovid Zeller, may his memory continue to be a blessing, tell the story of the man who met a *Lamed Vavnik*, I wanted to learn it so I could retell it. In fact each time I tell the whole story I can feel my throat getting tight and my heart filling up with emotions I cannot describe. Telling the story to Jewish people is easy, they either know the language or want to know more about their faith. I wanted to make the story universal, so I began making a mental collage of my various avatar-*Lamed Vavnik* experiences.

Of course there has always been Jesus, yet growing up I thought of him more as a threat to my being, as many Christians I encountered wanted me to find Jesus and be saved. As a nice Jewish girl this frightened me, because I was not grounded as I am now in my personal relationship with my G!D and my tradition.

Despite these fears, on my first trip to India I had a conversation early one morning with the statue of Jesus at the Sikh Gobind Sadan Ashram outside of Delhi. He "spoke" with me as his sister and I called him brother, and through this silent conversation I became clear about my mission to Israel: I would be meeting with Arab people to build bridges of understanding.

Then in Pondicherry I met the energy of The Mother, the spiritual partner of Sri Aurobindo. Sri Aurobindo was born in India and educated in England, and upon his return to India was a political activist for India's independence. During this period, he realized that the best way for him to bring about change for his motherland was to develop the spiritual practice. The woman known as The Mother came to Pondicherry several times from France. The stories about the encounter between her and Sri Aurobindo tell of a meeting destined in dreams they each had. When she finally came to live at the ashram, Sri Aurobindo went into silence and The Mother ran the ashram for about 50 years until her death. I felt that her energy kept me at the ashram until after her birthday. On the morning of the celebration of her birth, as I stood on the top of a guesthouse at dawn, I heard, "Yea, thou you walk through the valley of the shadow of death, I will be with you."

In South Carolina I enjoyed the "don't worry, be happy" energy of Meher Baba. In New Delhi I met Amma, the hugging guru, and can still feel her hug that I waited, sitting and standing for hours, to receive in a suburb of Delhi. Thirteen years ago I traveled to Pondicherry to experience the energy that Andrew Harvey described in his meeting with Mother Meera, and then last year I met her in person in Raleigh, NC, during a *darshan*. A Sanscrit word meaning "sight," during a *darshan* one is "seen" by the avatar. And then there was the dream in which I left my friends and was led into the mountains by an energy I knew was *Shechina*, the indwelling presence of the Divine. I later lived the dream as I walked a trail into the Colorado mountains, feeling Her Presence and a peace I rarely experience.

I am challenged to confront my mind, which likes to separate these people from the rest and not see the gifts of others I encounter. Who knows who the *Lamed Vavnik* really is? My challenge is believing that everyone is the Messiah and has the energy to heal their wounds and those of others, especially when I need to include me.

Spiritual Practice

When I recount the story of the rabbi who tells the abbot, "One of you is the Messiah," the emotion rises and I again choke up. Noticing these as teaching moments, when the heart opens to truth, is a reminder that I am at the right place and the right time, and I am at one with the universe.

Blessings of the *Vav*

When I include me with others. There is really no need to judge or separate me; the truth is that we each are unique and connected, and living the paradox of this reality. This is my practice as I heal my wounds and pray for the rippling effects of the tidal wave of loving-kindness washing over me. And I can breathe deeply, knowing I have again said *yes, and* to life.

5:34 AM

Tuesday, September 22, 2009

Surprises that Nurture the Soul

Photograph of TZiPi and Eleanor, taken by Phyllis

Blessings of Being Awake

I laugh as I type the words "being awake," thinking that it is way too early to be sitting at my computer. What brought me out of bed as I was watching my chest rise and fall and trying to get back to sleep was the thought that Robbie had found me through this blog. I met Robbie in Israel at a Thich Nhat Hanh retreat and she invited me to visit her home in Amman, Jordan, where she lives with her husband and son. I had just received a note from her, thanking me for continuing to write. Each time that thought crossed my mind, emotion filled my chest and bubbled. The joy of connection, of loose threads being gathered into the fabric of my life, create a foreground to my life's tapestry. I am a part of a whole that is my life. The emotion rises again, the tears fall, and I am happy through and through.

Spiritual Challenges

Thirteen years ago I said yes to the voice that told me I was going for a trip around the world. This summer I have had experiences — like Robbie — where those connections came back to life and I am now feeling that the dream is real. I took this trip, wrote about it, made connections that drifted away, and when I came back to NC, I went back to my life as I had known it. I drifted from home to home, not sure where I wanted to live, and added to my academic credentials — and below the surface of life the Mystery was working. I love surprises like these. I feel like I have been found and validated, and my challenge is to stay here, be nurtured, and just enjoy! I am a part of a life, my life.

Spiritual Practice

One foot in front of the other I walk though my life, a walking meditation, of paying attention to the gifts wrapped in various packages, and of letting things go and choosing nonviolence, of remembering to focus on the core of life-LOVE, of listening to my teachers who come in all sizes and shapes, and of continually seeking the Divine in myself as well as others. And most of all believing in me and my dreams, for they are good, they are very good.

Blessings of the *Vav*

Who knew my fascination with the Hebrew letters and language and taking myself seriously would lead to this blog. Devorah, my psychic friend and mentor, said that if I became a rabbi, and I was strongly resisting that call, I would also become a healer. I believe her now, as my heart's wounds are mending and its capacity is expanding. Who knew? She knew! We are all healers.

⌨ *4:53 AM*

Sunday, October 18, 2009

LOL

Spices at market, India

Blessings of Being Awake

I heard myself laughing with a burst of energy and I smile now remembering the moment. Miryam — a friend from my early days at Elat Chayyim — and I had been talking about our meditation experiences and the thought crossed my mind, "I can be the rabbi and practice Buddhist teachings and still be a good enuff Jew." I felt like I had been released from the straightjacket I was trying to fit into. "Either — or," I could hear the mind saying, "you cannot have both!" Is that really true? I wondered. I am a *Vav-nik* and I can have both. I can live the *and* life that I am trying to promote in the world. I am blending Hebrew wisdom and Buddhist practice in my life; why hide behind a facade of untruth?

Spiritual Challenge

I have to laugh at myself. I know we teach what we need to learn, and being a *Vav-nik* is more than passing out cards; it is actually doing the work, living the values I deem mine. Being alone, quiet, introspective is essential to my mental health and creativity. And in striving to remain in the world and honor the other part of me, I also need conversations where we share ideas, thoughts held close to the heart, rarely verbalized. I need to get out of my head the words that, when spoken, take on a different tension and have an energy and beauty that completes me.

Spiritual Practice

To remember the laughter so freely emoted and how wonderful it felt. To continue to believe in miracles and, like Sarah, I too can bring forth a child at 99. I can bring together opposing forces and find a renewed path for myself.

Blessings of the *Vav*

It is never over until the fat lady sings. I am not sure what that means and I do know I can continue to learn, expose myself to new experiences and collaborations, and not lose me, just most humbly deepen my relationship with the Mystery of Life.

7:58 AM

Sunday, October 18, 2009

THE GERUND

Veils Over the Soul

Blessings of Being Awake

Here in South Florida we have been waiting for the weather to turn so we can open our windows. And it is here, at least for now. Winter has come and I am happy to shut off the air conditioner. I can feel the cool breeze flow through my condo, front to back, bringing in fresh air. I take a deep breath, knowing change is happening.

Spiritual Challenge

To remember that whether I see change or not, there is always something brewing underneath the surface, and my impatience or hopelessness won't make it happen any quicker. The Buddhist teaching on impermanence and nonattachment, the Hebrew wisdom honoring teshuva, the right of return to the true nature, or — as I learned in Mark Epstein's *Thoughts Without Thinker*, the use of *ing* on the end of words — is a reminder that everything is a work in progress, including me. Change, change, change, I can hear the Mamas and Papas singing the song based on ancient writings. Everything is about change.

Spiritual Practice

When I feel tension related to change in my body, I will remember that breathing deeply is bringing the Life Force deeply into my hips and groin, releasing the fear that gets stuck in my throat. Hope is restored; courage and past experiences are reinforcing my forward motion, and a smile opens my lips, relaxing my facial muscles.

Blessings of Being a *Vav-nik*

Being able to sing full hearted the words from the song I learned as a child, "Row, row, row the boat gently down the stream, merrily, merrily, merrily, merrily, life is but a dream."

8:33 AM

Thursday, October 22, 2009

Early Morning Musings

Horse's skull, Cumberland Island, GA

Blessings of Being Awake

Yesterday via a webinar I listened to the author and coach Ira Chaleff talk about hierarchical relationships from a follower's perspective. I felt a kinship and wrote to him that he was a *Vav-nik*. This morning I received a note back telling me that the origin of his thinking is the Holocaust. I began to think I know where my fascination with the *vav* happened, and yet I was not aware of a core value that fed the real-time awakening. I am aware this morning that living a *Vav-nik* life is in opposition to some old experiences: living in fear of disconnection, my heart's *closed* default mode, and a familiar feeling of loneliness.

Spiritual Challenge

Studying *musar* with my *va'ad* group, we were talking about what *spiritual* means to each of us. Part of my definition is that I live as if I am in connection, in relationship with every person, place, or thing. I want a simple life, and yet simple is not easy. Staying in integrity with my values demands I stay awake. The other morning as I walked with my friends, I was bored with their conversation and left them in my mind. The next thing I knew I was down on the ground, bruised, glasses bent.

Spiritual Practice

How can I stay awake and put myself at the top of the list, as I support in my Facebook page, MULKA? I do not have a clue! I can only keep noticing my life with humor and gratitude, and be open to learning that comes in the most surprising places.

Blessings of the *Vav*

Yes, she is a blessing!

5:49 AM

Friday, December 25, 2009

MOVIES AS AN ANTIDOTE TO CHANGE

Stone sculpture of praying woman, Yucatan, Mexico

Blessings of Being Awake

I know this place I am in, as I have been here before. Life gets full of people and things and then — wham!!! Nothing will distract me from the feelings that arise. I am left to face the emotions I do not want.

Spiritual Challenge

To suck it up, let it out, be curious, and notice where I am without judging (usually impossible). To breathe and avoid falling into despair and hopelessness. To think about how I can cope in this moment and, as a last possible solution, to share my state with someone. To cry.

Spiritual Practice

No matter how alone I feel or how much I doubt everything in this moment, these are just thoughts. And the truth is that I also love me and I am good.

SO! I made a list of seven movies I wanted to see and I have now seen five, and today I will see two more. Yay for Christmas releases!!

Blessings of the *Vav*

We are funny people, a community of like others. Everyone goes through these feelings, adores being distracted from pain, and wants to give up. That is why the sages taught that I do not have to complete the work, and am I not at liberty to stop living the dream I am in (*Pirkei Avot* 2:21).

7:46 AM

Saturday, December 26, 2009

WE ARE NEVER ALONE IN SEEKING BALANCE

Close-up of rose with bud

Blessings of Being Awake

It was the third day of the silent retreat when I noticed a dull aching in the center of my back. My first thought was, "What made this happen?" and then the solution, "Maybe I was sitting wrong." Then as the mind wandered I remembered that it was a week and 13 hours since my mother was killed by the impact of the car, and maybe I was feeling the heart's pain. I reached for the small pillow I had brought from home, placed it right where the pain was centered, and leaned into the back of the chair. And with my next breath I noticed the tears coming down my cheek. I opened my chest, my heart wide, and rested in that moment.

Spiritual Challenge

Before I left for the retreat, my friend and hospice counselor, Miryam, had reminded me that I was in mourning. It was such a gift: a few words that gave me an anchored vessel to place all my feeling and thoughts within. These words were my connection to another reality as I floated in the dream of my life.

Spiritual Practice

Tender, tender, tenderness is my deepest desire for a default, when life gets so narrow there is not much room to breathe deeply. This space I offered myself — a week of silence — was such a gift, and one my mother had supported me in. About a month before her death we were talking about what to do for Thanksgiving, and when I told her about the retreat she had said, "Go. I have lived my life, you live yours." So I must learn to listen deeply to my heart and to those who love me, and never give up — for the next moment holds all possibilities.

Blessings of the *Vav*

I am a member of the virtual community *Agudat HaVav*, the Society of the *Vav*. I am never alone; I am Divinely connected to every place, person, animal, and thing. As I was reminded when I saw the movie *Avatar* this week; She does not take sides — Her deepest desire is for balance in the world. There will always be a moment, a word, a smile, an animal showing up to pull me back into balance whenever I go off kilter, for She is within me, my seeker of inner balance.

6:36 AM

Saturday, December 26, 2009

WHO'S GOT YOUR BACK?

Empty baskets, Aiken, SC

Blessings of Being Awake

It was Monday morning in the limo on the way to the airport, a few blocks from the hotel where my daughter and her family had stayed while we were in Boston to bury my mother's remains. Andrea said with much frustration, "Oh, I forgot to check out." I could feel my anger rise and before I could think, my mouth opened and a torrent of words burst out, not just to my daughter but to Urbie, Ashby, and Drew. I could not hold my composure and intention of love and kindness any longer. The pain of my mother's death — and that I was now the big cheese — overwhelmed me, and I wanted to know who was there for Andrea, for me, for us!!

Spiritual Challenge

It had been a long month filled with mourning, working, making plans, traveling, visiting, and honoring my mother's wishes. Now we were going home to the real world where my mother's physical presence no longer existed. I wanted to know who's got my back? Who will drive by my house to see if I am OK, as I drive by to see if she is OK, who will give me directions, ask me out to lunch, to attend a function, ask if I need bananas or bread or any kind of food when I arrive home from traveling or flowers for the Shabbat table or even to be a pain in the neck?

I had not voiced many of these feelings, for I could not admit the fear of the unknown that lay within me. I was in doer mode; I had a list of things to do to complete the mission. I had forgotten how important my mother's presence was to me, and I had no idea how much I was going to miss her presence and her place in my life. I would have lots of time to begin to see where I placed in her life.

Spiritual Practice

I have had the honor of working with several African American male clients, and each has voiced their distrust of others in the workplace, and how they have to have their own back. One of these clients also said of his God, "He's got my back." I like when clients share their faith with me, for it reminds me of what I already know: the Unknowable, Breath of All Life, does remain an integral element to all of life, including mine. I laugh out loud when I remember the story a teacher-sage tells of the agnostic who, in the passion of lovemaking, screams, "Oh, my god!" I, too, must allow myself to move in and out of my doubt when feeling alone. And I must remember that Divine Nature is within each of us, so we all have each other's back, strengthened by what I call G!D.

Blessings of the *Vav*

As long as I will breathe, there will be another *and* moment in which to smile, apologize, laugh, cry, celebrate, *and* the heart keeps beating on and on and on. As we are reminded when reading the Torah, where most columns begin with a *vav*, the stories are all interconnected to each other, affecting each other, transforming them as perspectives change with new information, and we are never the same after that. So is my life, and *Halleluya*!!

7:17 AM

2 0 1 0

Saturday, January 2, 2010

THE COMPETING COMMITMENT

Shy Flower

Blessings of Being Awake

Yesterday, Cousin Arnie called to wish me a Happy New Year and to catch up on each others' lives and our family's history. We were talking about our personal challenges this year and how, even when we want change, we often will still run into distractions that take us off our path. Since we are both in the business of making the world a better place, he is in HR and I am in coaching, I mentioned a favorite leadership development book, *How the Way We Talk Can Change the Way We Work* by Kegan and Lahey. The authors call the underlying cause of the distraction "a competing commitment." Working with this concept pushes me beyond my comfort zone to uproot whatever is holding me in place, and does not allow me to flow with the river.

At this time of year the secular calendar offers me an opportunity to pause and gain perspective on where I am and where I might have been distracted and gone off course. So this Shabbat morning I read in *Torah Queeries*, a weekly commentary on the Hebrew Bible written by lesbian, gay, queer people, and their allies, the *drash* for Vayechi (And He Lived), written by Rabbi Jill Hammer. This week's Torah portion about Joseph the outsider reminded me of a conversation I had several days ago at our monthly lesbian potluck. We were talking about the latest movies and someone asked if George Clooney is gay. I said I did not know. I then asked what is so toxic about being called lesbian or gay? There was a pause in the conversation and someone said she thinks Oprah is lesbian and will come-out after she retires. We all laughed, and I wondered out loud what would happen if being gay or lesbian was held in a place of honor or was just another adjective that defined a person? Eva responded that the world would be entirely different. I knew then what I wanted for myself more than any other gift for 2010.

Spiritual Challenge

I am committed to being politically correct, as it fits with a core belief of mine of being kind. Being careful with my language often keeps me from the opportunity of having deeper conversations, with myself as well as others. In *The Faith Club* the reason the authors' relationships grew in length and depth was because the women confronted each other on traditional beliefs that had not been explored outside these conversations. So for 2010 I challenge my need for deep connections, both with myself as well as with others, by asking these questions:

- Can I be both kind and truthful while being open to others, who confront me on my behavior?
- Can I speak my truth, as I did this morning with my daughter, Ilana, and deepen our conversation and my connections both with myself and her?
- Am I willing to share all of myself with others with pride and nonchalance, or even terror?
- Am I willing to do what the male lead in *Avatar* did: risk death to meet my partner and bond with another, to be able to fly together, blending energies and being the self of the moment? To risk everything to save a life, my life?

Spiritual Practice

Through my meditation practice and mindful living I am committed to uprooting and exploring the competing commitment of my intertwining of sex and emotional safety. To hold the image of my granddaughter, Etta Grace, as she freely dances in the water, smiling and laughing and being in joy with all of me, so stunning in all my true colors everywhere!

Blessings of the *Vav*

In the mystical tradition of Hebrew wisdom, the vav resides in the body and holds the energy of emotional connection. I am feeling the erotic nature of this energy, and reveling in the aliveness. I am aroused and smiling with joyful innocence and delight of the possibilities this holds for me.

10:53 AM

Monday, January 11, 2010

IF DOING IS BEING, WHAT IS RECEIVING?

Fire

Blessings of Being Awake

My friend Ana Tampana's call this morning reminded me again that I need to just be receiving and healing. Her words sound true and echo the same words a friend gave me last week: You only have to receive. At that point I drew my third drawing expressing my grief: a picture of a huge heart filled with grey color and little red hearts floating in and out and around her, and some even touched her edges. As I drew the hearts that touched my heart, I viscerally felt the tenderness and soothing nature, and I wanted more. Yet, I am not practiced and I am awkward at ministering to only me.

Spiritual Challenge

I want to move on and I feel stuck in this bedlam space. I need to stay here and learn how to care for me, the one who has set an intention of creating more art space and less intellectual space. I need to listen to my heart and words of intention, and to walk with the great fear into supporting me in my dreams, previously set aside for the universal fears of success.

Spiritual Practice

Today my friend Roberta — who has come from her home in Asheville to visit her mom and friends in South Florida —and I will clean up my office so I can walk around the past and potential creativity that now looks like boxes and books. I will say goodbye to all that I have held on to that made me feel safe, protected, and gave me an identity. Oy vey!!!

Blessings of Being a Proud Member of the Society of the *Vav*

To walk the talk of being a vav I need to stand tall, openhearted, strong back, being all of who I am. And in the present moment I need to be inspired to follow my heart, which can only be heard in the stillness of silence, as Ezekiel's experience reminds me: Be still, and only then can you know G!D.

10:47 AM

Thursday, January 14, 2010

And Eventually You Become the Matriarch

Cousins, 1947

Blessings of Being Awake

On November 11, 2009, at about 6:15 in the evening, I became the head of my family, consisting presently of two daughters, their husbands, and four grandchildren. This was not my decision, like becoming a parent or taking on couple responsibilities when I got married. On the day my mother quite unexpectedly died, I became an orphan. There is no one beside me or behind me to be the final decision maker, the one who holds together, the glue. I am it! And I am not even sure what *it* is, although I may have seen it from a distance. I was not prepared for this new role, even though I did on one occasion try to imagine what it would be like when it did happen. I could not!

Spiritual Challenge

I feel like I am out in space without my spacesuit, untethered, looking down on earth and hoping it stays very far away! Am I ready for this role? How is it different from before, as single mom without a partner? How will my relationship with my family change, or will it? I wonder how the Godfather felt when it was his turn to take over. I am excited about wearing the purple robes of royalty. And I have lots of questions. One thing I will remember is to stay in touch, keep them up with my plans, and learn a lot! That is my challenge as a fiercely independent, hippie, only child, woman of the world.

Spiritual Practice

When my mom was alive she covered for me. I could travel, miss calls, never get to calls, and without knowing, she filled in. She had a relationship with my daughters that I will never have, as each couple has its own energy. When Pharaoh said, "Go, and leave the women," Moses responded, "We must all go together, as we will not know how to serve G!D until we get there." So why worry about the future? Phyllis Ott, the only person still living at the Meher Baba Spiritual Center in Myrtle Beach, SC, reminded me today that her spiritual guide, Meher Baba, taught "don't worry, be happy." Maybe that is what this matriarch will do, since I am sure this death, which laid this role in my hands, was not my idea and was already in the plans. I am not sure if I am ready to take it on — and I will!

Blessings of *Agudat HaVav*

I have the blessings of being a member of the Society of the *Vav*, a *Vav-nik*.

At the top of most columns in the Torah there is a *vav* at the beginning of the word. The sages tell us that this means the story is ongoing; we only stop to take a breath before we go on. So for a while, as I move through the grief, I will remember to breathe, as I cross this threshold and enter my new role. I am sure that my ancestors, the Ivrites-Hebrews, the "boundary crossers," as Rabbi Gerson Winkler names them, knew how to stop and breathe and remember to be grateful that they were never alone. And I am royally receiving the energy of my ancestors in my new role.

2:31 PM

Monday, January 25, 2010

Afflicting the Comfortable

Lotus Beginning to Bloom

Blessings of Being Awake

I laugh with myself as I think, "I am a sign watcher," like the main character in Coehlo's *The Alchemist*. When I hear a phrase more than once in different contexts, or I see a pattern of information coming my way, I think, "Oh, I need to pay attention, this is for me."

Since my mother died and my daughters and I emptied her home, I have taken on the task of simplifying my life and home. I have been digging through the boxes hidden in the back of the closet, reviewing my life through the things I have held on to and no longer need as a reminder of an amazing life. When I came across my ordination certificate, I stopped and read it. The wording is clear and powerful and reminds me of my charge. The words, "Comfort the afflicted and afflict the comfortable," had been sitting quietly in my mind.

And then yesterday, when I was listening to Jay Michaelson speak on spirituality, I heard him say the same phrase. For me these twice-repeated phrases were in alignment with my visceral awareness and connected thoughts that say, "It is time to go deeper and push the edges of your comfort zone." Naturally, as I put this all together, I want to know what it means and where I am to practice this afflicting. I want to imagine what I cannot imagine, so I can be the captain of my ship and director of my home movie. And, deep breath, I have no idea what this afflicting will look like or where it will happen.

Spiritual Challenges

Last week's Torah portion involves the continuing saga of the dueling dialogue between Pharaoh and his hardened heart and Moshe and his uncircumcised lips. At one point Pharaoh said to go, but only to take certain people. Moshe countered with, "No, as I will not know how I am to serve G!D until I get there." This phrase has been so helpful to me. It helps me notice when the mind is plodding away, and to stop planning and practicing before it is my turn to speak. It reminds me to listen and be in the moment. When I remember that I truly know nothing, I understand this is a moment to support my desire to strengthen the mind to stay Here and not to wander, creating a safety plan of just-in-cases. Now, this moment, is the only place I have any control over. My mother's tragic death and her upcoming 92nd birthday are vivid reminders of that truth.

Spiritual Practice

So again I am sitting with the *kavana*, the deep intention of my heart, to learn and then practice how to afflict the comfortable; to go deeper and to not let being politically correct keep me from deeper conversations, and to be transparent and honest. To help me have what I want: an open heart that includes me. I only have to love me as if I were my own lover, I do not have to take care of people who can take care of themselves.

Blessings of the *Vav*

I can continue to open my heart to include me, to notice the fear and work with it, not run from it; to notice that under the fear is a tender heart that only wants connection to herself, to others, and her Divine nature.

10:57 AM

Tuesday, February 23, 2010

The Meeting of Peace and Reconciliation

Mourning Heart Being Touched

On the 9th of Adar, about three months after the accident that took the life of my mother of blessed memory, I met in the lawyer's office with the woman who drove the car that hit my mother.

I did not think of this meeting as an act of forgiveness, as it is not my place to forgive. That is between her and her G!D. However, my intention was to offer her information about my family and how we are coping, tell her our perspective on what happened, and let her make the decision about her own suffering.

This was a meeting whose general intention was for peace of mind and heart, and reconciliation with our hearts, which might be wandering, alone, distraught, feeling abandoned and bad — why else would such a horrific thing happen if you did not deserve it and were being punished?

My daughters and I had wanted this meeting, after all the legal decisions were finalized. We had heard through the lawyers that the woman was distraught and all of us wanted her to know us. We viewed what had happened as an accident, and we were grieving deeply for the death and our loss of my mother and their nana.

The meeting went well, and there was transformation. I would describe the conversation as an I-Thou encounter, using the German philosopher Martin Buber's description of a meeting of the souls.

It was awkward at first; no matter how much training I have, crossing the threshold into the unknown is often slow and cautious. I said my usual prayer, "*Ma yakar hasedecha, how precious is your loving-kindness*," to assure myself that I was not alone. I wanted conscious recognition that I needed Divine Presence, I could not and did not want to do this alone.

We talked for about 35 minutes and went from knots to flowing strings, from politeness to authentic warmth. Toward the end of our time I held her hands and sang to her my rendition of Leonard Cohen's *Hallelujah* that had been ringing in my ears.

"We will do and we will understand," the Hebrews say to Moshe. Sometimes you have to do something even though you do not know why and have no agenda or imagined outcome. That is how I felt about this meeting. And now that it is over, I am pleased with my trust in my sense of rightness and courage to follow through. I was very brave to meet with the woman who drove the car that hit my mother that led to her death. My bravery led me to know me in a deep way. I had circumcised my heart in public, and my hope is the world is a better place because of these moments in time.

When I came home, I dressed in warm and comfy clothes and drank hot tea and sat on the floor reading over the condolence cards that were sent to my family. I wanted to be close to the people who knew my mother, and I cried deeply and spoke to my mother's Spirit that I was sure was comforting me.

Blessings of the *Vav*

I could not have done this if I had held to a right-wrong, good-bad, way of thinking. I would still be in a vicious cycle of not knowing, and connected to an image of a woman I would never know. I could only have known a blessing today with the teaching of the *vav*, and trust that not knowing is an OK place to be, with the support of my daughters proving that this only child is never physically alone, and knowing that my Mother, of blessed memory, is always with me, cheering me on in her silent unique way. I am sure that being a *Vav-nik* allows this heart to know love. Maybe this hope I hold on to with such tenacity is not unfounded.

7:38 AM

Monday, March 8, 2010

I Am Smart
Just by Asking
the Questions

Doors

Blessings of Being Awake

Where did they go, asked my adopted sister Phyllis, after the camps were liberated? It was early this morning when room service brought the coffee and tea. I had not wanted to get up, and there I sat wrapped in the terry robe, sipping my hot water and eating freshly cut fruit, talking about deep questions as we celebrated Phyllis' birthday at the St. Pete hotel.

When my friend and colleague Mary Lynne made the decision that she was not going to be a living-walking-on-this-earth being by taking her life, she reactivated in me many emotions and thoughts related to life and death and the choices we make.

When my mother decided to walk across the eight-lane boulevard not at the crosswalk and met a car, she changed how I looked at her life and a paradigm shift began to happen within me.

Spiritual Challenge

I want to stay awake to living on the edge of not knowing. I want to stay fascinated about how opening a door, walking around a corner, crossing a threshold, having a thought, can change one's perspective and behavior. How can I keep the door open to possibilities, continue asking the questions, and not just accept what is and move on? My sister Phyllis is a good role model for asking the questions.

Spiritual Practice

What does one do early in the morning with these deep thoughts that stir the soul and mind with wonder? Keep asking them and not needing to find the answers.

Blessings of the *Vav*

Asking the questions is important, knowing the answers is not. *Vav* allows me to ask without knowing the answers, so I can stay curious in this abyss of life. And....

11:40 AM

Tuesday, March 9, 2010

Choices

Emotions

Blessings of Being Awake

When I got up to relieve myself early this morning I thought it would be easy to go back to sleep. We had gone to bed late after a full day of new experiences, meeting people, dancing, and exploring the ship, where we would spend the next five days. Yet the rolling of the ship and the vibration of the motor left me restless and awake. I kept moving from side to side, trying to find the perfect placement of my body that would invite back the deep sleep and great dreams I had just been embroiled in. I was angry at the boat, our room, and the designers of this ship that kept me awake.

Spiritual Challenge

It is easy for me to respond to the angst of the mind by joining with it and making up all kind of stories. "Yeah, you're right, we were done wrong, I will never get used to this movement, I will stay awake forever," were some of my more dramatic thoughts. I took a deep breath, listening to the voices, and thought, "I am not going to play this time!" I started breathing deeply and was aware that in my angry place I was tight. I was holding the tension I had just had a massage to relieve. I laughed, silently, not to awaken my sister, and then began to notice that as I breathed I became more relaxed, and instead of being a board torn by tempestuous seas, I was rolling and following the rhythm of the boat's movement.

Spiritual Practice

To remember that I am *shalem*, whole, and a symphony of separate parts: one very busy mind, one wise body, and one very alive spirit living together with the Indwelling Presence. And we all must learn to live with each other. We are in relationship with each other and in any relationship there are moments when tension is high and flow is limited. Yet, this is also a moment of potential freedom of working together for the greater good, to be at our highest good. Each moment can be an inspiration.

Blessings of the *Vav*

In every moment there is a possibility to move beyond the habits, rather than remain in my old comfortable rut. In each moment I can call on the *vav*, the emotional connector, to help me find what comes after I say *and*, and go deeper with knowing what my unique soul can be.   **10:33 AM**

Wednesday, March 10, 2010

Going Deeper with the Words

A narrow street in Italy

Blessings of Being Awake

He looked about my age and came with his wife to my meditation class. From his speech pattern I assumed that he was either a *sabra* — native-born Israeli — or had learned Hebrew at a very young age. His tender heart asked me a question: "Would you mind answering a question, and you do not need to answer if you do not want." I knew I would tell him anything he wanted to know.

"What do you mean when you say, 'meditation saved my life'?" he asked with a curious, sad tone. As I started to talk I felt awkward, as if I was walking into the unknown. My thoughts rambled; one time I knew the answer to those questions: What does it mean? What am I willing to share? How vulnerable am I willing to be? Who am I talking with? Who would understand what I experienced that is so hard to put into words?

Then I remembered those 10 days in Thailand that brought a peace within me that I had wanted, and yet did not know how to access. My teachers, Rosemary and Steve Weissman at the international meditation center, Wat Kow Tahm, had created an emotionally safe environment for me to learn about Buddhism, a process of thinking that I would utilize for my whole journey around the world. It would bring me to moments in which my heart was softening, firing the embers of choosing life and wanting more.

Spiritual Challenge

I casually said to him, "I am still alive and I am here telling you my experience." He smiled as we looked at each other. I then spoke these words, "I am learning to love me so I can love the stranger within and without." And he smiled again and spoke the Hebrew text, *and you shall love the stranger as yourself.* We smiled and let the others in the class know this teaching of Hebrew wisdom. Truth comes when the right questions are asked.

Spiritual Practice

To breathe deeply and go within, remembering the Divine dwells there — in my body, with me — and never leaves. I am never alone. Healing is placing myself back into my loving heart. That is how I save my life, breath by breath, moment by moment.

Blessings of the *Vav*

When I stand with the intention of authenticity and the thought that nothing can stop or kill me except myself, then I am able to link with another who is in that same place. I am making a step toward mending the world.

11:10 AM

Thursday, March 11, 2010

Being Distracted

Rainbow

Blessings of Being Awake

"So you lost both your parents in the last two years — that is a lot, especially for an only child," a new acquaintance said in response to my telling her how I ended up in Florida. I was so pleased that my sunglasses blocked her from seeing my eyes well up as my throat tightened, and I did not speak as we turned to focus our attention on getting organized for the kayak expedition.

Spiritual Challenge

My neck is tight, my shoulders have rocks in them, and I miss my mother. I get a massage for the shoulder pain — what do I do with these feelings? I wonder about how I can remember the gift of unconditional love she gave me, and let that soothe the ache that arises spontaneously in my heart.

Spiritual Practice

Taking time to be gracious with myself by mourning and grieving for this primary relationship. I have committed and set an intention of creating an art piece in her memory. She would love that a lot, since she too was an artist.

Blessings of the *Vav*

Being able to hold the pain of loss and the joy of our relationship, as all is truth, the whole story. So in her memory, I will show pictures of the cemeteries I visited while on the March of the Living with my grandson, Ashby, in Poland. I am holding the pain of loss and the joy of being alive! *Kaddish: A Tzedakah Project*, the YouTube video my friend and brilliant photographer, Janice, and I will create together, is a work of art, honoring the awesomeness of life given.

9:12 AM

Friday, March 12, 2010

And G!d Was in This Place and I, i Did Not Know

Weeping Heart

Blessings of Being Awake

As we relaxed under the Mexican sun, my new friend, Alexis, spoke her wisdom into the group, "Women are naturally competitive." Everyone agreed, and I had to catch my breath. I had never thought of us in that way. I know my aunts are competitive with each other, my mother was competitive with me, and my daughters are competitive with me. Yet, I had never thought of it as a characteristic of all women. I spent several days musing on her words becoming lighter, no longer weighted by "just me" syndrome, and more enlightened with each breath.

Spiritual Challenge

Feelings of competition and envy are the reason I asked Phyllis if we could adopt each other as sisters. Not knowing this for sure, yet having a sense that competition is normal between siblings, I wanted to do something with these competitive feelings that were interrupting my end of our friendship. I love Phyllis like I love my daughters and I love my mother, and I know the many times I sensed the presence of competitive feelings and steered around them, never exposing them, always letting the walls remain between our hearts. In my writings on Sarah for my ordination, I remember expressing in a poem the toxicity of competition with a need to get to know her deeply, every crevice, so competition could stop running my life.

Now, having a perspective that these feelings were female-relational linked and not just mine was so freeing. I felt as if someone had just cleansed an opaque windshield that prevented me from seeing the whole picture. In this moment my soul felt cleansed from the toxic energy that keeps me in judging mind and separated from my sisters everywhere!!! I felt as if I had found the holy grail for which I did not know I had been searching! And I wondered how I can hold on to this truth and not let it slip through the cracks of life.

Spiritual Practice

Laugh; what else can I do but laugh at my-our competitive spirit, and then laugh some more, no longer constricted from seeing my own beauty by these feelings. And then remember the wisdom from various traditions and wise ones: do not covet, be the best you that you can be, your success is your deepest fear, do your personal best, and consider the idea of power *with*, not power over or under, as Starhawk teaches.

Blessings of the *Vav*

In Hebrew wisdom we are told we carry two notes, one in each pocket. One note says, "I am just dust," and the other, "The world was created for me." This interpretation of humility, "knowing your place and taking your space," is untying me from past thinking and behavior. No longer strangulated, I am empowered with this information that can only save my life and perhaps that of others. And I am so glad I was listening as my new sister-friend spoke truth into the wind and I heard and wove her wisdom into my being. May I continue to live the truth that the Divine lives within everyone, and I can learn from everyone, including me. I am a *Vav-nik*, standing tall in my uniqueness and hooked to every other *Vav-nik* healing our world!

6:51 AM

Sunday, March 14, 2010

Endless Exciting Dreams

Flowers

Blessings of Being Awake

In Greensboro a few weeks ago I went with my friend Gay to a wonderful art show called *Embodying*. "Yes!" I said to myself as I walked around the art space, inspired by the amazing, creative, and daring artists. I began thinking about my unfinished projects at home and how to pull them together. I'm going to introduce the quilted circumcised heart with the paper mache bust! I felt the excitement of new beginnings and thought, "Art, that is my new love!!"

Last week on the cruise, a new friend, Geri, needed some health support. I offered to do some energy work and to use some new healing cream on her sore places. As I rubbed the cream into her skin, she commented how good it felt and asked if I was trained as a message therapist. "No," I smiled and said shyly that I had gotten that comment before. I love choosing the people I touch for healing and thought maybe that is where I need to put my energy! I could study and be a good massage therapist.

Before I went on the cruise I facilitated a coaching skills group and got high on collaborating with the men I worked with. It was fun and I came home thinking I need and want to do more of this!! And I began thinking of how I could expand my practice and do good in the world.

Spiritual Challenge

When I first came-out I bought a T-shirt that said, "So many women — so little time." I was just beginning to imagine what I would *do* with all these women and I certainly appreciated the idea!!

Now I am feeling, "So many loves — so little time." I want to go deep with the time I have left on this earth. I want to be good at one thing and be noted for it, and I want it to be something that gives pleasure and energy to people as it heals them and me.

I have so much to learn to be able to do that. What shall that be? I ask myself. What am I playing with already that needs to be opened further, like the vagina upon giving birth? What am I about to drop from my womb? Who will I be, where will I live, who will be my lover or friend? So many unanswered questions, so much to learn. How do I discipline the mind?

Spiritual Practice

Today the question arises, tomorrow another piece of the puzzle will arrive. For today all I have to do is be in receiving mode! I am noticing my heart opening and tears falling, emotions high. To notice without judging myself, just expanding into the love that is already there holding me.

Blessings of the *Vav*

Whether hidden or revealed, the *vav* sparks an unendingness to life and pushes the game of wonder from the back burner to the front!! It is boiling and I cannot avoid the reality!

11:29 AM

Sunday, March 14, 2010

Taking the Crap off the Soul

Up close, a flower

Blessings of Being Awake

For two days I have been crying and wiping my nose! I am not crying all the time and yet when I do start to cry it is deep and long, and I am coughing up whatever I have been holding in! It must be purging time! Spring is here and love is around the corner.

Spiritual Challenge

I am walking in the confluence of two streams: the deep dark night of the soul and the eternal light of a pure soul. I know that what I am experiencing, major unlovableness, relates to the grief around my mother's death and her feelings of unworthiness that I am trying to peel off my soul. It is not the whole truth so I am not giving in to self-doubt, just watching. I must admit I am also trying to figure out how to get through this.

Spiritual Practice

This is the moment I have been practicing for. I will call friends to cry with, just for them to listen. I will sit outside and get some sun. I will take a bath and soak in the water. I will only care for me, as there is no energy for anyone else right now. I will love me as I make my way through the darkness that covers parts of the soul. I will breathe deeply and hold on. The rollercoaster has just hit the top of the hill and I will be coming off my seat as I hold on for dear life! And I will hold on.

Blessings of the *Vav*

This too will pass. I am making a friend of time. There is deep learning here, a hope that maybe I can speak from an authentic place to help someone else through their dark, dank, and narrow place. And all of this is love!

⌨ *11:40 AM*

Monday, March 22, 2010

I Need to Sleep with Competition

Tree limb, Negev

This poem was written as a weaving of the study of Sarah, the first matriarch of Hebrew wisdom, and my spiritual autobiography.

I need to sleep with competition
I want to know her intimately
her curves, lines and jagged edges
Her ins and outs
The dark hidden places and those that protrude

I need to embrace her, love her
for unless I really know her
she will constantly be there, ready to trip me up
make me small and limit my possibilities

I need to clean myself of the sin of
Adam who thought he was not good enough
to eat the fruit of the tree of knowledge

I need to heal my self
from the pain of separation Cain felt
from his brother as he compared
came up less and then destroyed a part of himself

I do not want the pain of your envy
to constrict my heart
to keep me from seeing the beauty
of the One who held me before I was born
who loved me before she knew me
whose heart was broken by the one
she trusted to care for her and all she loved.

Dear Sarah, what was it like to compete
with your sister-friend Hagar for God's gift to each of you?
What happened and has never been mended?
Was it the man who divided you because
he did not know how to love each for your unique gifts?

Or was this God's plan all along — we were
never to do it right — only learn from
life and missed opportunities.

Blessings of the *Vav*

We are all One, connected to each other, impacting, responding, blessing, intruding.

⌨ *5:17 PM*

Tuesday, April 6, 2010

A Retreat in the Moment

Energy Movement

Blessings of Being Awake

I had an amazing moment this morning that I want to remember, so I am writing to get clear with what happened! As I sat in meditation, I noticed a feeling that I can only define as refreshed, an experience I have had on long silent retreats. The feeling lasted for quite a while; even now I can conjure the emotion up and I smile. Delicious!

Spiritual Challenge

To keep doing and being, while remaining open to the surprises that gift me — like the sweet orange blossom aroma that wafted my way last week driving through central Florida. The traffic had slowed down and I felt stuffy in my air-conditioned car. I wanted some fresh air, so rolled down the windows. What a sweet aromatic delight!!!

Spiritual Practice

Keep being faithful to me by setting aside the time in the morning to just sit and focus on the miracle of a body that breathes all by itself. Today I sat by the open windows, connected with the natural world, listened to the birds, and felt the sun on my body as my chest rose and fell with each inspiration and expiration. Maybe I will know that the Divine Holy One of Blessing is in this place and that I am Home.

Blessings of the *Vav*

In traditional Judaism we count 49 days or sheaves of wheat called *omers* between the second day of Passover and the giving of the Torah on Shavuot. In mystical Hebrew wisdom we do this with the intention of refining our soul so we can receive the Torah as free people worthy of this holy gift. Each week and each day focuses on an emotion or characteristic associated with G!D. This first week is lovingkindness, and yesterday was bonding.

Loving-kindness is getting easier for me to hold, especially with myself; and bonding has seemed foreign and unlearnable to me since I began this practice several years ago. Yet, in the practice of being a *vav* and holding on to an *and* mode of never giving up, always having hope, and knowing that this too will pass, I still held the intention for 24 hours that I might have some insight into how to bond. I think today I bonded, and the Most Holy One of Blessings was there. I took my shoes off my feet and saw the burning bush that was not consumed. I heard my name called and tears flowed as I arrived at an awesome Place I never thought I would experience. And in this moment I said, "*Halleluya*," knowing that sometimes you can only know the Divine after She has visited.

9:23 AM

Thursday, April 22, 2010

Intro to the *Kaddish*: A *Tzedaka* Project

Wild iris, Israel

In the spring of 2007, my grandson Ashby and I participated with hundreds of other teens and adults from around the world in the March of the Living. We spent one week touring and experiencing Poland and one week learning Israel. On our first day in Warsaw we visited the Jewish cemetery and as I walked silently through the winding rows, I found I had wandered away from the group to the edges of the cemetery. I came across many tombstones that lay one atop another, on their side, and in ravines covered with dead leaves, vines, and debris. Our leader had told us that many of these cemeteries were not being kept up, and yet this area felt more lonely and forgotten. I felt a deep sadness as well as a righteous anger.

When I returned back to the USA, I was aware of a deep need to honor my journey and those victims of hate who had been abandoned. For many years I had stood to say *Kaddish* for all those who have no one to honor their memory. Yet, because of my experiences in Poland and Israel, I now understood and recited the words that praised the Work of the Divine with feelings and images that connected me to these lands and people.

In the fall of 2009, it had been a little over a year since I had finished the 11 months of saying *Kaddish* for my father (of blessed memory) when my mother suddenly and tragically died. A week after her accident I was traveling for work and alone in a hotel room. I felt lonely and, in my grief, compelled to recite the ancient rhythmic chant, the Aramaic words that I had been speaking with my daughters, neighbors, and friends the previous week. I know that traditionally one says the *Kaddish* in the presence of a *minyan*, 10 men. Yet that has not been my custom and, as I stood by the window looking at the sun setting and began reading the words that I had come to know so well, I hoped my G!D would understand that my intention was more important than the rules.

As I spoke, I sensed the room beginning to fill with the energy of souls dressed in the winter garb of the people of Eastern Europe during World War II. I was in awe and deeply moved and comforted by Presence. I felt soothed by their compassion and remembered the truth that I am never alone.

Blessings of the *Vav*

In those moments I became aware, as others before me, of the power of the words of this prayer that honors transitions that occur during death. *Kaddish Yatum*, the Mourner's *Kaddish*, is a prayer said by the "orphan" with the intention to remind the heart and offer a paradoxical state to the mind that, in the midst of grief and sorrow, there is an amazing world that we inhabit. For me, consciousness is being awake and is the first step toward healing my broken heart. If I can hold both the grief and the joy, only then is healing possible for me.

⌨ *1:36 PM*

Friday, May 14, 2010

YES, AND

Rainbow

Blessings of Being Awake

It is so important for me to notice my allies when they show up! Today I got an email from my colleague and friend Chuck about the cast of the comedy show Second City doing an exercise with a management group in Germany where they played with the concepts of *yes, and* vs. *yes, but*! And they enjoyed the process.

Spiritual Challenge

So many thoughts flashed through the mind when I read his words. The one thought I chose to hold on to was an Ethiopian wisdom quote: Many spider webs coming together can tie up a lion.

Spiritual Practice

I often forget I am not alone, ever! And when I do I usually trip over my feet. I am beginning to learn that seeing the sparks of G!D in everyone and everything is like getting a hug from the universe and feeling loved and seen and known. My neighbor Connie would say — and I would agree — "can't get any better than that!"

Blessings of the *Vav*

In a rush to mail each of my daughters a card, I did not seal nor put a stamp on them, and somehow the cards were received. When I half do a task, sometimes there is an entity, we call her Nana, who makes sure my back is covered and I feel so blessed. May everyone be so blessed.

Shabbat shalom! Blessings of a sweet and renewing day, and *chag sameach*, joyous holiday blessings. May you be at the right place at the right time to receive the Word.

12:28 PM

Wednesday, June 2, 2010

Do You Talk
with G!d?

Banyan trees, West Palm Beach, FL

Blessings of Being Awake

Another opportunity arrived to try something I encourage others to do: talk with G!D.

Spiritual Challenge

So, I wonder, who is G!D? Where is this G!D I want to talk with, to? I usually say G!D is good. Well, is that true? I am a Jew, I wrestle with G!D. Which G!D? Outside, inside, female, male, a blade of grass, a bird flying by? How can I focus on one?

Spiritual Practice

Breathing deeply, I smile and decide not to suffer as I go back to creating with paint, stamps, and fabric. Praying that the Divine Source of All that Is, the One Without End, will shut down my mind and flow through my hands, creating beauty, reflecting my soul.

Blessings of the *Vav*

Only when I am standing tall in all that I am and in all my possibilities, not suffering more than in that moment, remembering that I can choose life and joy. *Yes, and* I am living a *Vav-nik* life.

11:49 AM

Saturday, June 26, 2010

And the Children Will Lead Them

Etta Grace

Blessings of Being Awake

While focusing on my life's mission I checked this blog and noticed I had not written in a while. So I am making time for what grounds me in the now and honors what I love doing, expressing myself with the written word. It is Shabbat and I am working on my laptop, which does not have all my photos on it — and I wondered what image would be available for me to use. As soon as I looked at this picture of Etta Grace — which her mother, my daughter Ilana, had taken — I could feel the rightness of the choice in every cell of my body, especially in my eyes, which yearned to release the tears of knowing that I am at the right place at the right time.

Spiritual Challenge

To transcend boundaries the mind creates around right and wrong. To hold on to my innocence or, as the sign at the airport said, "Dance like no one is watching." To be the *neshama*, the pure soul I took life for, and continue to honor her journey. To focus on what brings me joy and find joy in what I do every day. To remember age is only a number and everyone can be my teacher, that suffering is not an option, and that kindness to myself is my core value. To laugh at me and with me.

Spiritual Practice

I am making time for my creative projects and interlacing them with my cognitive work, knowing they feed each other and therefore me. I am remembering that I can practice anywhere and use different tools to create. To notice the judger voice and say there is no right or wrong about me, all is me, and sometimes I am just not patient, kind, and loving. And it is perfect, as the kabbalist would respond, in the physical world. As I move through the world and practice accepting all of amazing me, it will be easier for me to live with others.

Blessings of the *Vav*

I can always pause and look in the mirror, face to face, and say YES! You are fun to be with!

1:47 PM

Sunday, July 11, 2010

INSPIRATION: SEEING THE GARDEN THROUGH THE DOORWAY

Japanese garden, Society of the Four Arts, Palm Beach, FL

Blessings of Being Awake

Learning for me has to be on my terms. I learn, like my teachers the Baal Shem Tov and the Buddha, by my own experience. Too often in the past I have felt like a failure trying to fit into someone else's system, as in repeating the fifth grade because I could not get the multiplication tables down, or in grad school in quantitative statistics when I just could not get the concepts. Deep breath!! Here I am again on the edge of learning something really big, and it involves all of me, head, body, spirit. I am learning to be consciously vulnerable with people who I think need me to be strong. I cannot hold my suffering in to myself any longer.

Spiritual Challenge

I need to believe and trust that this learning will benefit the world; that what I am practicing and getting good at is not just about me. I need to remember that while I am saving my life and uncovering my pure soul by bringing me back into my heart, I am also living a life knowing I am unconditionally loved by the *Ein Sof*, the One Without End, and connecting with all there is that is being loved. There is no hierarchy of who is loved.

Spiritual Practice

Deep breathing in, expiring, emptying all doubts, creating space for holding me and the pain of separation from the universe. Sitting in meditation knowing that this still time is building a relationship with myself. I will be laughing out loud at me for trying so hard to be perfect. I am taking the advice of two wise people: Dr. Nicholas Vacc, of blessed memory, was chair of the counselor education department at University of North Carolina at Greensboro, where I completed my doctoral work. He once told his Ph.D. candidates, "Settle for a B." And Patricia Ryan Madson, who in *Improv Wisdom* instructed readers to "be average."

Blessings of the *Vav*

I am no longer staying in confusion. I am more clear what my path is, so the *but* is being left out fairly frequently from my vocabulary, as it is with my friends and clients and colleagues. And as I become more clear, my world opens up and I am feeling the blessings of the Unconditional Lover. Yes *and*, I am ready to cross the threshold into new learning.

11:31 AM

Monday, August 9, 2010

"Love Is All You Need" Is Not Enough for Me Today

Falling Down the Rabbit Hole and Coming Out Alive

Blessings of Being Awake

I noticed the passion in my voice and excitement in my body as I talked on the phone with my friend and colleague, Cheryl, yesterday about my interpretation of the concepts Adam Kahane wrote about in his book *Power and Love*. Kahane expanded on Martin Luther King's and Paul Tillich's writings on love and power while telling his story with great vulnerability and inquiry of his work on social change. I told Cheryl that a book had not excited that much interest in me in a long time; I had written and drawn all over the margins, the notes invoking thoughts and emotions and a lot of *vavs* and *ands*. As I ranted on, I got clearer about how important these two energies are for me. The Beatles' lyric, *"Love is all you need,"* has been my mantra; loving myself as if I were my own lover has been my intention. Trying to figure out what that exactly means has been my practice! In this moment, I am aware that the missing element to loving me is power, the generative energy to grow my soul.

Spiritual Challenge

Living as an only child, introvert, solo-no partner, I have ignored the love, the generative energy of connectedness and unity. My challenge is to learn how to live the paradox of *I* and *we* simultaneously. Oy vey, just writing those words makes me nauseous! This must be a large threshold to cross; I am making the transition to the other side, feeling the power and the love.

In the movie *Invictus*, Morgan Freeman plays Nelson Mandela. In it, he reads the last few lines of the poem *Invictus*, which gave him inner strength during his imprisonment. I wrote them on a sticky note and stuck it on my computer, and they inspire me forward, "I am the master of my soul: I am the captain of my fate." I link them together with the words Hillel wrote, "If I am not for myself, who will be for me? If I am not for others, what am I? And if not now, when?" And I am empowered by those who came before me.

Spiritual Practice

In my workshops on visioning, storytelling, and strategic planning, I use the phrase, "Together we can make anything happen," and I often remember my father's famous line, "We need each other." I need the mind, even when it separates me from others. I must value my body, which holds all the emotions and sometimes cannot do every yoga move; and I must remember my Spirit, which I can feel even though it is not physically seen. I need you as you need me to be complete, individual, unique, and connected. My practice is to live as if I am one, interdependent, intra-dependent, fulfilling my soul's mission to grow and heal the world for us together.

Blessings of the *Vav*

The letter *vav* exists with its own intelligence and has the holiness of the mystical energy of connectedness. She stands between heaven and earth, within the emotional torso of me, the third letter of the One Without End. And I am circumcising my heart, loosening the thickness of my neck, and coming home.

9:15 AM

Sunday, August 15, 2010

A New Name, a New Relationship

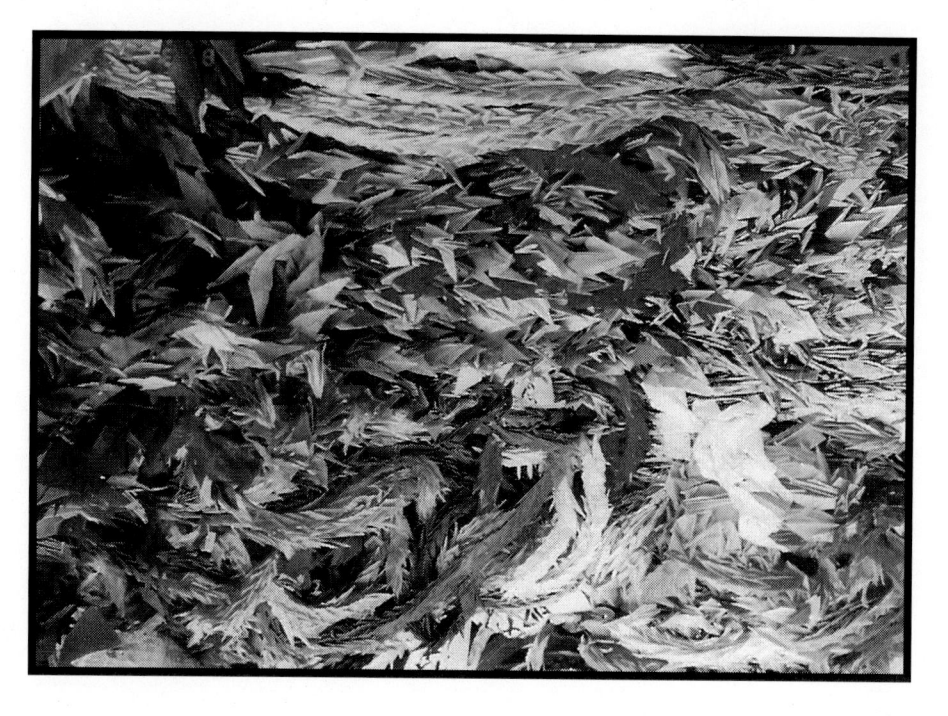

Origami cranes at Peace Park, Hiroshima, Japan

Blessings of Being Awake

In this most holy month of Elul, when we blow the *shofar* every day to remind us to wake up and come back to our true self, I am choosing to focus on something to prepare my soul and being-ness for the new year, 5771. I have chosen to change my relationship with the three-letter word for the Mystery of All Life, Blessing Bestower. These three letters, g-o-d, have lost their luster with me and have become more problematic than supportive and loving. There is an emptiness when I say this word. And now that my parents are dead and I am an orphan, I must truly take care of me because there is no one else to do this. And I am viscerally aware of becoming more alive. Rabbi David Zeller, of blessed memory, sings of believing that this aliveness is G!D. I have chosen a name for this Divine *Ein Sof*, the One Without End that is Unending Love, which empowers me and speaks to my wholeness. For now the name is *HaRachamana*, the Compassionate One. And I am smiling.

Spiritual Challenge

To remember that I am holy and I am *HaRachamana*, without judging myself for forgetting and falling back into old familiar patterns of doubt. To remember that I can hold me as *HaRachamana* holds me, and I can empty my body of anything that is not needed to be held any longer. Letting me back into my heart and my womb, and as mystical Hebrew teaches, I am being the androgynous giver and receiver that I am.

Spiritual Practice

Breathing in the name and noticing my visceral reaction; breathing out the name and noticing my body's response. *HaRachamana* lives within for those moments I am awake and even when I am asleep, walking through my life.

Blessings of the *Vav*

There is no end to what the mind can imagine, and if I connect the dots, all the dots, I can begin to feel included in the 10,000 things, no longer an outsider. When I listen to me, the *HaRachamana*, there are only possibilities.

10:13 AM

Wednesday, September 1, 2010

Collecting the Dots of Being Gotten

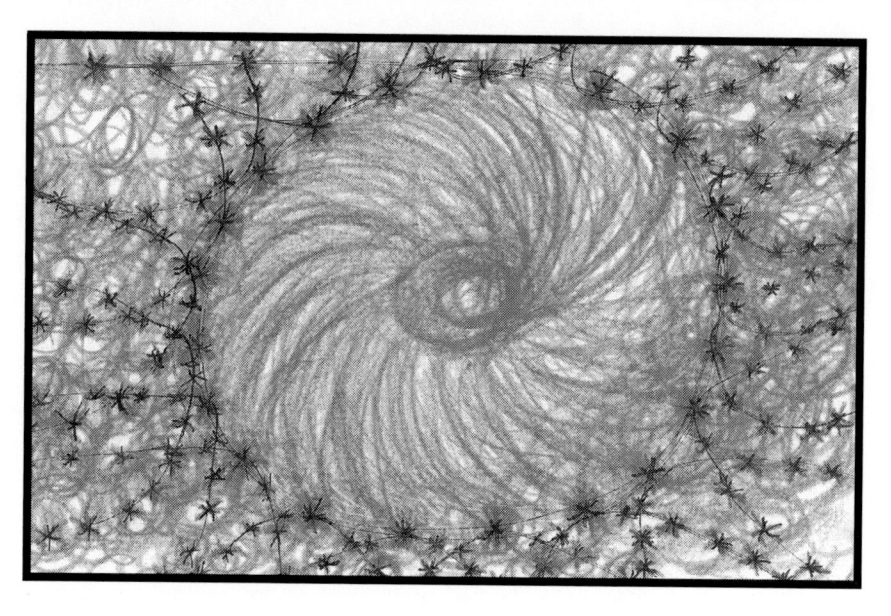

Divine Sparks Creating the Universal Force Field

Blessings of Being Awake

There have been moments in my life when I feel I have been *gotten!* There was no need to try to be anyone else but me. I felt the tenderness, the acceptance, the joy right down to my core that did not need to hide, be politically correct, or hush-up. Those are rare moments when I have met someone who knows me better than I know me, the self that walks too often in fear, loneliness, straight-jacketed.

Staying home this summer, making my travels purely domestic, has offered me the opportunity to open my heart to me and the struggles of relearning how to love me. I am remembering those who knew what it was like to be different, who found me in the crowd of their life and bestowed their kindness in their joy of finding clan.

One of the dots I am collecting is of poet James Kavanaugh, author of several books including, *There Are Men Too Gentle to Live Among Wolves*. Kavanaugh came to Aiken, SC, to share his work in the early 1970s, thanks to my friend Beverly, who arranged for his visit. He was my family's guest for dinner and conversation. The evening was filled with love that my guest made sure I received. His gift was of being seen with *chesed*, lovingkindness. My body still remembers the delightful surprise. And my dear Buddhist therapist, Tim, reminded me the other day that being mindful of the experience in one's body-mind-spirit is the gift we give ourselves to help us *get* ourselves! And to experience the experience, I must be awake.

Spiritual Challenge

I am beginning to collect the dots, the moments, the experiences, when I was gotten; to name them and celebrate those courageous souls. What I am beginning to notice is that what I learned from them unconsciously, I am passing forward. And I do, when I am kind, laugh at life, ask for a name, listen to a story, cry with someone, offer to sit beside someone in their pain, celebrate the joy of a triumph. That is my job, and my life's work is to learn that what I do for others I must do for me, too. I know loneliness too well. And I have been touched by the light, the *ner tamid*, eternal light of these holy souls.

Spiritual Practice

I often say, "I am blessed," when strangers ask how I am doing. I say it not because I am feeling blessed in that moment. I do it to remind me of the blessings bestowed upon me when I was not even looking. By collecting these dots, I am collecting the blessings of the many experiences I have been gifted with by the souls who *got* me. And in this holy month of Elul, I am asking them for forgiveness for not telling them *thank you*. I am forgiving myself for not noticing the light they so generously shared with me.

Blessings of the *Vav*

James Kavanaugh died on December 29, 2009, without me telling him *thank you*. I will share this blog entry with his family. The *vav* is so holy in holding the linking energy and individuality of the self. I have been blessed to listen to my heart, which sits in the emotional state of the body, and honor the words that came to me by creating this blog. There is a Society of the *Vav*, and it is coming alive like me.

8:00 AM

Monday, September 6, 2010

COMINGS AND GOINGS OF ETERNITY: MEETING AGAIN, STILL TASTING DELICIOUS

Eternal Movement

Blessings of Staying Awake

Today my friend Mary Ellen called from Canada. She reminded me of "guest consciousness," a phrase that arose while I was a guest at a home in New Zealand. Mary Ellen has been using the phrase frequently, while I had forgotten it.

Spiritual Challenge

To remember that whether I am birthing from the womb or birthing from the heart, each is a holy offspring that needs to be nurtured. "But no one listens," is not an option. I need to listen. I need to listen!

Spiritual Practice

Make a list of the ideas that have come through me and honor them somehow!

Blessings of the *Vav*

I have fallen in love with *and* because I want to de-*but* the world. First, I have to de-*but* my world and begin noticing how often I say, "Ya, but!" to my birthings. And LOL!!

11:39 AM

Tuesday, October 5, 2010

Reminders of the Joy in Being Me

Two found objects, Peru

During my Vision Quest preparation and debrief, our guide — my friend Alicia — taught us to pay attention to what nature is trying to teach through her many and varied gifts. On the Santa Cruz trek I had asked the mountains to offer me insight on the pilgrimage I was about to embark on. Here are two cherished gifts for which I am still allowing the knowing to evolve. This is where I sit today.

On the afternoon of the first day of the trek I was walking with Del, one of the other hikers, and responding to her curiosity and specific questions about what happened to the sacrifices in the Old Testament. At one point I was distracted and looked down to find a piece of wood that looked just like a bird. I quickly picked it up and carried it carefully as a treasure. I conveyed my excitement to Del, explaining that in Hebrew my name means "little bird." Discussing the sacrifices, I told her that the root of the word for "sacrifice" is *korban*, which means "to bring close." After the destruction of the Temple in Jerusalem the rabbis created prayer services, contemplation from the heart, to create the opportunity that the sacrifices offered. Those prayer services are now moments to be close with the Divine three times a day.

On the third day of the trek, Del's husband, Len, and I had gone for a short walk in which he was coaching me to slow down, take baby steps, be totally in the present, and use my breath carefully and deeply. Our conversation related to many things, including my mother's death and the grief work I was still doing. When we came back to camp, I approached my tent feeling ready for the next day's walk up to the highest peak. As I bent down to unzip the tent, there was a huge stone in the shape of the heart. I feel a connection to heart shapes and quickly placed it inside the tent to be carried with my gear. I was taking this home, no matter the weight!

This morning as I told the story of finding the heart stone to my friend Chuck, I spoke about my first attraction to the text in the Torah: "Circumcise your heart and don't have a stiff neck." I need to circumcise my heart, remove the covering, learn something new about me — or, as it says later in Deuteronomy, "The Divine will circumcise it for you!"

Spiritual Challenge

To notice the gift and go deeper than the physicality of what presents itself. I will try to notice when I judge a book by its cover, because if I never open it I may miss what there is inside that will nurture my soul. I want to remember that everything has a spark of *Ein Sof*, the One Without End, in it. I want to continue to believe that I am worthy of the gifts, and keep turning them over until I find the essence.

Spiritual Practice

I will keep telling the story until I unpack the secret message just for me. Today I am honoring my choice of using the Hebrew word TZiPi to introduce myself, and to take pride in my connection to the tradition that continues to feed me. What I did naturally is who I am. I am unburdened and free to be the me that I am.

Blessings of the *Vav*

We are told in Hebrew wisdom to "never stop doing" while "knowing we will never finish." There will always be a *yes, and* moment, another opportunity to see a different point of view, to gain perspective from someone or something else or even myself. The River of Light is endless and flowing. I am learning how to swim!

11:56 AM

Satruday, October 9, 2010

NATIONAL COMING-OUT DAY: SMILING AT FEAR

TZipi and Phyllis at the 2010 Valentine's Day Sweetheart Ball for the Sonia Plotnick Health Fund, St. Petersburg, FL

Reflections on National Coming-Out Day, October 11

Blessings of Being Awake

In 1977 I met my first Jewish lesbian and fell in love. Today we are still friends and still in love enough to keep working on our relationship. I was just coming-out as a woman loving women. I was recently divorced, a single mom, and a second-year occupational therapy student. There were so many new experiences; I had so much to learn, so many trips and falls, and so many fears that I could neither name nor face. There was so much I did not know that I did not know.

Spiritual Challenge

- Laughing with myself as an act of self-love as I begin to notice, then let go of, the fear of not wanting others to know stuff about me — when the fact is they already do.
- Remembering that loving another is often easier than loving oneself, and that when I do not love myself there is so much pain. Although I have practiced since 1995 to treat myself as if I were my own lover, I am still a beginner.
- Accepting myself in all of who I am. Being the oldest I have ever been, with all those physical changes I do not like, takes a maturity and perspective I know I do not always have! Despite these challenges, I will keep heading toward the unknown, as it is an act of love. As the Hebrews spoke, "We will do and then we will understand."
- Learning that coming-out is a moment-to-moment self-discovery experience. My coming-out must be done with love and a commitment to my soul's mission. Therefore, I hold the Torah's teaching that the One Without End, the Compassionate One, is holy, and so too am I holy.

Spiritual Practice

To smile and remember that I am made in the image and likeness of the Divine. I am amazing most of the time and sometimes, as my Uncle Harry, the Doc, of blessed memory, would say, a jerk. I breathe deeply and say, "I am holy, sagging boobs, varicose veins, wrinkled face, gray-haired wizened one." I cannot hide from the unending love within me, nor do I want to hide from the mirror. I am good, kind, and loving, even when I wonder about that truth.

Blessings of the Vav

The *vav* reminds me it is never too late to face the fears and come-out. In the movie *Unconditional Love*, Kathy Bates is a great role model of the bravery of a warrior. I ordered the shruti box, a small wooden box that makes droning sounds to use while I am making voice sounds that Deborah, my voice therapy coach, taught me. I am coming-out as an experiential learner. I am experimenting with the Divine, being at one with all my fears. I am smiling at my fears as they evaporate. I am enjoying myself, my shruti box, my sounds, and this life gifted to me.

May your coming-out be blessed, too!

10:28 AM

Friday, November 5, 2010

HALLELUYA, PRAISE THE ONE WITHOUT END

Fall leaves, New England

Blessings of Being Awake

Sometimes being awake is not fun. I wrote this poem after a Sunday of being the only chaplain in a hospital in Greensboro, NC. It was a day full of many challenges. When I reread the words of this poem, visual and visceral memories arise — from the newborn in the NICU, whose mother sat beside the incubator, confused, watching her child struggle to hold on to life, to an elderly woman whose husband sat beside her crying as she took her last breath. At the time, I was more easily using the familiar word for the One Without End, god. Today, this word feels flat and I want a more active word for the Never-Ending Love.

Also, at the time, I was finding my identity as a Jew. I was discovering that the word I said in Hebrew, *Halleluya*, was also being said by my sister and brother Christians, Praise God! I was living in the Bible Belt, where these words rolled off the tongues of the people around me. I felt those words were their language and, if I said them, I would be less Jewish. I laugh as I write this, thinking that we are such funny people with our small minds. I felt uncomfortable speaking their language, especially with the same intensity. In writing the words of this poem, I was getting used to their language, trying it on for size, making it mine, learning from them what I did not think I knew: that *HaRachamana*, the Compassionate One, the One I desperately wanted to know, had saved my life for some purpose I have yet to understand.

Praise God for creating home
    Even when we cannot find it
Praise God for bringing us home
    Even when we do not know when we get there
Praise God for spitting us out
    Even when we are not ready
Praise God for catching us
    Even into awkward hands
Praise God for each breath, tear, sigh
    Even when we are embarrassed by the emoting
Praise God for the voice that sings your praise
    Even when out of tune
Praise God for every life you take
    Even when the anger exacerbates the pain

Praise God for each life you give
> Even when we cannot appreciate your miracle

Praise God for the resiliency modeled
> Even when we cannot get unstuck

Praise God for the vulnerability we often experience
> Even when we are shamed into silence

Praise God, Praise God, Praise God!
> Why not praise God

Better than damning the pain in my heart
For all those whose grief I witnessed today.

Blessings of the *Vav*

And I will always have another chance to make another decision, to relook at the decisions I have made. Hebrew wisdom teaches me that I always have the right of return, *teshuva*, returning to my true self, to be true to my soul's journey. I want to continue to grow the *mochin de'gadlute*, the big mind, to gain perspective, to give myself the time to learn what an amazing soul lives within me.

8:16 AM

Sunday, November 7, 2010

Getting the Whole Picture

Hole in tree trunk

Blessings of Being Awake

As I walked into the quickly filling clubhouse auditorium last night, I saw Edie, a woman I have known since first moving to Century Village. She was looking around as if she were waiting for someone. My heart got excited as I walked over to greet her. I have loved this woman from our first meeting in the workout dressing room when I moved to Century Village. She had lived in Israel for many years and loved to speak Hebrew with me, as I with her. She loved to sing in Yiddish and was so full of fun and joy. She endearingly called me Tzipila. Yet, this woman I kissed and spoke Hebrew with last night was engaged in make believe. She called me by a name unfamiliar to me. She looked blankly in my face and appeared cautious. A thought crossed my mind, "I think Edie is pretending she knows who I am, as she does not want me to know her confusion." I remember seeing that same look on my father's face as his mind began to atrophy.

As I left her to find my seat, I remembered the picture I had taken of her last November. She was standing at the voting entrance holding the sign for Obama over her head with a big smile on her face. I imagined that as her family went through her things, they would see this picture and remember this other time when she was full of life. I felt full of many emotions, wanting to hold this whole picture, the variations of her life.

Several weeks ago in Miami at the "Adventure in Intimacy" workshop led by Hedy and Yumi Schleifer, Hedy talked about having many marriages, then paused to add, "to the same man." What we were seeing that weekend was another incarnation of their relationship. So when Yumi said that in one of those marriages he had been a jerk, I had to remember the plethora of roles I have also played in my various relationships. And I had to welcome myself back into my heart and forgive myself for all the expectations I have that make me my enemy. "I am my friend, my best friend," my mother used to say to me.

Laughing out loud I say to myself, "I am being forced by various experiences to hold multiple realities, each holding truths." Not only am I expanding my lungs through being at very high altitudes and breathing deeply as I sing with my shruti box, I am also expanding the mind, proving that old dogs can learn new tricks and fulfilling my mother's comment, "You are my Einstein."

Blessings of the *Vav* and Ecclesiastes and Solomon

Believing in the transformation of the soul, in its many seasons, while holding the variant colors of possibilities, is having faith and hope in something bigger than me, the Mystery of Life, the One Without End, the Compassionate One.

8:58 AM

Thursday, November 18, 2010

JUST BE YOU

Flowers

I look at these flowers and I wonder if they ever doubt themselves, compare their bloom to others and come up short or feel desperately alone. And then my tears start doing their thing as I laugh out loud remembering, "I just need to be me." Isn't that what I have been practicing all these years? Just do it your way and it will be right. It might not get me an A by someone else's standard, and no one else is grading me but me! "Just be average," I hear Patricia Ryan Madson, my *Improv Wisdom* guru, saying — and I know my "average" is amazing!

Blessings of Being Awake

Tonight I will have an hour to impart my joy of Hebrew wisdom and meditation to a group that is paying to learn from me. My emotions vacillate between being anxious and being relaxed. I want to do it right; my intention is to be improvisational and learn while having fun. I am reading some new information and remembering all my classes and my own practice. I know whatever happens in that 60 minutes will be perfect and direct from my heart, which sits in the body that holds wisdom.

I feel grounded in my experiences and the many people who have imparted their wisdom to me. I have learned directly and indirectly from many people, and to them I dedicate our time tonight: Stephen and Ondrea Levine, Steve and Rosemary Weissman and students at Wat Kow Tahm, Thailand, Abby Karp, Thich Nhat Hanh and everyone at Plum Village, France, Joseph Goldstein, Rabbi David and Shoshanah Cooper, Rabbi Sheila Perltz Weinberg, Rabbi Jeff Roth, Rabbi Joanna Katz, Sylvia Bornstein and all my teachers at the Insight Meditation Center in Barrie, MA, Rabbi Jonathan Omer-Man and Nan Fink, and Richard White, Beth Lynn, and Brett Ferrigan and students at Shambala House in West Palm Beach, and many others yet to be named.

I have practiced by myself, reading books, driven by something I did not understand. I have been given instruction and space to learn. In Thailand I walked away knowing that the teaching had saved my life. I have taught others and they were appreciative. Today is different. I know nothing and I know everything I need to know. *And* I am saying *yes* to the invitation to show up. And whether it is because there is no one in between me and the Divine, or because I am finally living that there is something bigger than me and I am paradoxically surrendering while being an active partner, I am showing up.

Listening to the inner voices led me to the Society of the *Vav*, which led me to this *yes, and* exercise in improv. There is no time like now, *hayom yom*, this day, this moment to continue the saga of this life. I am doing it, *ahni*, I, TZiPi Radonsky, woman in all my permutations of roles. And I am in joy!! Come join me, so we can play *anachnu*, we, together.

⌨ *1:26 PM*

Thursday, November 18, 2010

It's My Job to Be Me

Etta Grace

Etta being Etta: We have so much to learn from our young ones who are determined to be themselves!

Blessings of Being Awake

"It's my job," she said with great pride and ease when I thanked her for being so naturally out as lesbian. "Its my job," I repeated to myself several times as I walked away from Alix Dobkin, singer, songwriter, author. What a role model and sister collaborator, I thought. She is inspiring me to continue on my path of self-love — a path I am not sure I could be walking if my mother, of blessed memory, were still alive.

Spiritual Challenge

To find the edge and then to leap. I am learning to know and stay true to my core beliefs, and then to walk the talk, to live as if I were treating myself as my own lover. To do this I must stay connected to the moment and to the One Without End, who wraps Her Self around and inside of me, forever faithful, protective.

Spiritual Practice

As always, to breathe deeply, expanding the narrow spaces anxiety brings. When I go within, I am led by the One Without End, *HaRachamana*, the Compassionate One, down the path of righteousness. "Be proud of your differentness," I hear my heart saying. "Enjoy your outsider status, you are *kadosh*, separate, unique, you. Enjoy yourself, it's later than you think!"

Blessings of the *Vav*

As I evoke the sixth letter of the Hebrew alphabet within me, I walk between heaven and earth. I am a connector, a hook, a holy priestly letter. I am standing erect in my own uniqueness, ready to connect. What *chutzpa* it took to listen and then validate by giving attention to the thought "Society of the *Vav*" so it could grow! Nothing new for me, if I look back on my life. I have been here before and answer *but* to my ideas. This time I am integrating those moments as I write another chapter in this holy life I have been given. What is your amazing miracle story?

9:51 PM

Friday, November 19, 2010

Rushing off to New Things with the Wisdom of the Past

Wisdom of the Past collage, India

Blessings of Being Awake

Many years ago when familial depression was a regular visitor, I remember making a commitment to myself. Each time I felt useless, internally stuck, helpless, with no energy to do anything, not being able to see beyond my nose, I would remember my ancestors who were in concentration camps, and say to myself, "I am only bound by the limitations of the mind. I have more choices than they did." My sorry-for-myself moment would shift a bit to help me see other options.

Earlier this week, I found myself not being able to find passion and interest. And yet, like many of my ancestors, I kept moving through the day searching for the light that might appear at any moment. Last night's meditation class was a very bright light. This morning, after meditation , I pulled the Daughter of Wands card from the MotherPeace Round Tarot deck. I felt the earth/fire energy and knew I was "integrating the wisdom of the past" into the present moment.

Spiritual Challenge

I am committed to the intention of seeing myself as a whole person with a rich, full past integrated into my present; a part of both heaven and earth, never alone and therefore connected to many souls and being influenced by them as they by me. When I traveled solo around the world, an important piece of wisdom came to my consciousness: I am matter and therefore I matter in the world. I could no longer think of myself as unattached, a hungry ghost searching for redemption.

Spiritual Practice

I renamed myself with the name of the maternal great aunt I was named after, Faga Tubie, the good bird. I use the Hebrew version to remind me of my Divine connection to *HaRachamana*, the Compassionate One. Like Jacob, I have two names, one given me by my parents and one chosen for me by the Never-Ending Love. Introducing myself with that name is the most natural experience for me. I believe it was the name I was known by before I was born.

Blessings of the *Vav*

The story is never over, just continues from generation to generation.

Andrea took on a new name, Simcha, as joy is what she feels in the work she has chosen. May we all be blessed to wrestle with the Divine and find our Self.

9:26 AM

Sunday, December 12, 2010

The Importance of Being You, Honoring Difference

Yellow six-pointed flower

The beauty of nature repeating itself and each time never being the same.

I think I may be getting boring. Friends would say that is impossible. Maybe I am redundant, saying the same thing too many times! Yet, obviously, the mind I live with continues to stay with one thought until I get it. And sometimes I am sooo slow!

This morning's meditation brought me to thinking about the importance of being yourself. The Society of the *Vav* teaches that only when you stand upright in who you are can you hook up others. Who really wants to be alone? Even in the Torah it is written that it is not good for humans to be alone. As a coach of leaders, I know that collaboration is essential to making the world a better place. We are in desperate need of partnerships, of courageous followers who will speak up and over and down to all they work with.

Recently I listened to a taped conversation between a gay man and Abraham, the entity that Esther Hicks channels. I have been pondering on their thought that being different and being out encourages people to deal with their own angst about difference. I like the thought of being a catalyst for opening eyes and hearts. In *The Dignity of Difference*, Rabbi Jonathan Sacks writes that we all come from the same source and evolve into our own unique holy selves. In Hebrew wisdom, holy means separate, unique, discrete. Kahlil Gibran wrote about the coming together of two souls for love, about the winds of heaven dancing between the oak and the willow. I hear in his words the importance of being your unique self, and dancing together with the Divine's blessings.

And yet the mind loves to compare and judge those different from us. And we either come up short or better than the other. This is no way to build partnerships.

If the Torah had only written in the positive what it said in the negative, maybe people would learn 'not to covet your neighbor' but to honor your own gifts. Appreciative Inquiry teaches that what you give attention to will grow! "Do not covet" means we are already doing it, so what can we do that would put the energy into making relationships work? In their couple workshops on intimacy, Hedy and Yumi Schleifer teach about building bridges to the holy, sacred space where the past remains in the past and the present offers opportunities to listen and to hear; to mend the hearts that yearn for connectedness, to let down the wall a bit, to welcome the stranger as yourself. To learn and know her or him and yourself within that moment.

I say let us give attention to learning how to connect, not separate ourselves from each other by building walls around us, by comparing and contrasting. Let us learn how to have a growth mindset, as Carol Dweck writes, in contrast to a fixed mindset. And I ask myself, what do I want to learn? And can I be a learner in the now?

Enough rambling!!

We cannot hide who we are; that only encourages others to not have to face our own differences.

As a Jew, I am not going to hide. G!D made sure of that — circumcision for one thing. Different way of praying, different Sabbath day, different holiday schedule from the majority Christian community. The Nazis would also say big noses, and so do our Middle Eastern neighbors!

So I wear my Jewish star earrings with pride, yet always telling the story how I got them. They are a gift from my Christian friends who found them in India.

As a lesbian who is not in relationship, I can pass. My black friends or other people of color cannot pass. So how can I be out?

Dialect and pronunciation will expose one, like the people from South Carolina I met on the beach yesterday. Pass as what? I ask myself. As one of them, not to make waves and not to stand out?

As a woman, I felt I had to be careful of what I wore so my breasts would not distract from what I was saying. I am over it! I am on the cusp of 70, so just be me! Wild woman!

We are such funny people! I can only laugh out loud at me!

9:04 AM

2 0 1 1

Sunday, January 2, 2011

I Think I Am Falling in Love with G!d!

The Good Fence, Metula, Israel

Holding the paradox of real life: hard and soft, sharp and sweet, cold and warm, at the Israeli-Lebanon border, the Good Fence, in Metulla, Israel.

The other day, I heard and felt a voice that thought about falling in love with G!D. It felt good. It felt good right in the middle of my body, expanding my heart, just a little bit, with a sense of joy. I was shy about it and let it be. Then I thought, "What would my friends say if I told them I was falling in love with G!D?" My adolescent voice said, "Who cares!" Maybe I need new friends. And how many would think I was strange? They do already! I laughed out loud at that thought.

Then, when I started to ponder the idea further, as my interest was piqued, I tried to figure how to fall in love with G!D. Of course, this mountain in front of me is my responsibility to climb, to determine what falling in love with G!D really, truly means. Then I started to feel awkward and inept, as there must be only one way of falling in love with G!D. And I, poor me, did not know the "right" way to do it! All the ideas that started to flow into my consciousness sounded not good enough, in my estimation. They were ideas like, "Become Orthodox." As much as I love structure and order, that world is too far one way for me. I want an interfaith, multi-racial, multi-generational community. Like Brooklyn!

Then the thought came, "Maybe I do not have to figure out how to fall in love with G!D. I can let G!D tell me, show me what G!D needs from me. Then that G!D will know that I am in love with G!D."

Then I thought, "Get simple, basic." I am made in the likeness of G!D and maybe all I have to do is love me and that would be loving G!D. Then I wondered if I was being blasphemous. I have to do it right, you see, to be good. Now this sounds convoluted and a little unsure of myself. And that is just where I am now in terms of my relationship with the One Who Hardens People's Hearts and Who Is the Compassionate One, Who Is Without End, being what god will be. I was trying to invoke the Lovingkindness of the One Who Connects Us All of a three-letter word.

I do not believe there is a personal G!D and yet I do have my own personal relationship with the Source of All Blessings. I wonder what the difference is? I decided this is academic and one-way thinking. How can anyone prove that their way of loving G!D is right or wrong? There can be as many ways of loving G!D as there are people on the planet. And maybe G!D may not be the word some use, preferring Source, Higher Power, the Light. There are so many languages that describe this energy that is nowhere and everywhere. I do not think that any of those words involve violence, greed, killing, abuse, dishonesty, or disconnecting. I know it is painful for a seed to burst forth through the earth, or animals that kill for survival, or giving birth as the head reshapes itself and the vagina widens and the womb pushes the infant from its cocoon.

So, I will continue to seek and be open to receiving the feeling I felt when the thought arose within me. Maybe it is around the next corner, maybe I am on the edge of fulfillment, soon to find the missing piece of the puzzle, and the doorbell will ring and someone will offer me a million dollars for winning the lottery for falling in love with G!D.

Laughing out loud, I place my head on my pillow, hoping that sleep will come. Then I, like the seekers before me, will dream sweet dreams of finding home, knowing we will wake in the morning refreshed and reunited with the soul we took life for, ready to seek fulfillment again and again and again.
As you see, I will never complete the puzzle until my life is over. And only the One knows when that is — maybe. Who knows and Who ain't tellin'! So here I go again, walking the path of my deepest desire, swerving off and on, always returning to open my heart to love.

⌨ **10:29 PM**

Sunday, January 9, 2011

I Am Yearning for the Familiar

Etta Grace behind the wheel

And the child will lead them: As she steers the boat, Etta Grace's joy has reminded me of my leadership commitment to joy as I am leading myself back to Home — my true self — yet again! LOL at the never-ending learning life I have chosen!

I have been away from my physical home for five days now and everything is new: people, food, room, bed! Even turning on the faucet is a learning experience! And I do not go home for four more days of newness!

So much new and I feel grounded and flowing as I continue to be mindful and to do my rituals of chanting and meditation. The work I am doing is good! I am being creative and myself. And yet, I am feeling like I am missing something. And there is no one I want to speak with, no one but me to fill the missing-ness.

So I pulled out my iPod and began to listen to the music and I noticed the tears falling down my cheek as my heart began to open again. Oh, that is what has been happening, I have covered my heart! I have disconnected with a part of myself. I have managed to avoid the other feelings that arise when I am traveling and excited about the adventure.

The people around me are loving and I am not receiving that love, as I am in a back-up, armor-on stance. I am the cat that feels unsafe and the woman who is missing the familiar. Oh, *Halleluya!* for these quiet moments of self-discovery! I am eternally grateful for solitude taken and self-love given.

The joy has been there all along; I have not been in alignment and I have forgotten my commitment: stop, listen, and reflect. And now I will go for a swim, laughing out loud at, and with, myself. Returning home is a moment to celebrate!

10:19 AM

Thursday, January 20, 2011

We Need Each Other and Together We Can Do Anything — Yeah, But

A palm grows in Jamaica: Growing can be messy and beautiful.

As my mind wanders through this blog posting I notice that I need to come back to the beginning and give attention and a focus for what I am trying to write about today.

I am focusing on three ideas: 1) noticing the *buts* I say under my breath that keep me from staying on the path of my intention, 2) the importance of engaging others in my process as sustainability partners, 3) seeing all this as treating myself as if I were my own lover.

And so I begin again:

I laugh at myself as I write the title of this blog. The very word I have been avoiding is right in my face and lives with me every moment as I live my mission of de-*but*-ing the world by substituting the word *and* for the world *but*!

And I laugh out loud, knowing I teach what I have to learn!

The many years that my father of blessed memory was president of the synagogue where he and my mother were members, he concluded his announcement of events at the end of services with the phrase, "We need each other." I am not sure when or how it came into his consciousness to say this, whether it was being the youngest member of his family or just seeing how divisive we can be. We thought it was great! The phrase became a mantra for his whole family, including my daughters, Andrea and Ilana, and myself. The gated community he and my mother lived in even picked up the phrase. There is a sign by the exit that reads, "We need you, buckle up!" And for all his saying the phrase, sadly, I am not sure he believed we needed him by the end of his life.

Several years ago, I had the opportunity of working with some young people who were fellows of the Acumen Fund. Jacqueline Novogratz is founder and CEO of this nonprofit venture capital firm. I was given her book, *The Blue Sweater*, to read and to learn how a woman's belief that "together we can make anything happen" can change the world. I loved the phrase, as it seemed to take "we need each other" another step forward. I used this phrase in my visioning and storytelling workshops with women, encouraging them to think of themselves as leaders of themselves. At the end of the workshop, before they shared their vision and story, we set up accountability partners to keep them on the path of their vision.

I ponder who my accountability partners are.

I am seeing that I am blessed by many. I remember in preparation for my trip around the world, I gathered some friends to put up the map of the world. They kept me honest in following through with my dream. When I was having my *bat mitzva*, I gathered my friends to ask them to support me by arranging the food in celebration of that Sabbath. Asking for help, exposing myself to needing someone, is very hard to do.

And where am I going? I am headed toward uncovering the *buts*, the "competing commitments," as Kegan and Lahey write about. The competing commitments or, I would say the *yeah, buts* leaning on the big assumptions, that the mind thinks it knows better than the heart and keeps me in fear of change. The *yeah, buts* that keep me in old patterns that I think have kept me emotionally safe in the world. This is my short list of *yeah, buts*:

- yeah, but what would they say
- yeah, but they won't like me
- yeah, but I do not think I can do it
- yeah, but what will people think
- yeah, but I have not enough money
- yeah, but I am not smart enough
- yeah, but what about my family, I need to think of them too
- yeah, but I won't do it right
- yeah, but I do not have time
- yeah, but it would take too much time
- yeah, but it wouldn't make a difference

I am frequently aware of and often experience the desires in my heart. And the yeah, *buts* are so subtle, quiet, sneaky! I have to laugh at myself and say a thousand *ands* for each yeah, *but*!

I am fascinated by the many times I hear from people, "Why can't I do what I know I love or want to do?" or "Why do I know what I need to do and cannot follow through?" A teacher of mine, Marc Gafni, talked of "standing at the edge of fulfillment." What is it about that moment that thrills me so much that I do not want to leave, so I just stay there?

I also ask myself when I am going to let go and just do it, be loyal to myself, as I am to my clients, who tell me that I keep them honest. When am I going to be loyal to me? Tantra teaches the joy of sitting on the edge, holding the tension before the climax. And my voice teacher tells me to stay on the edge of emotion and ride the edge! So I am getting to build a relationship with the emotion of the edge, and I am going to ride! Yahoooo!

Yesterday a client told me of something she wanted to do, that she knew would be good for herself. As we explored and unpacked her desire to the last detail — when she would do what she knew she loved and had avoided — I committed to thinking of her at the moment that she would begin on her journey. And I got this note from her:

* At 1:00, part of me was arguing, "No, don't go. You don't have time. It's more comfortable to stay where you are." Another part was saying (more loudly), "I have already stated my intention to walk at 1:00, and TZipi will be thinking of me walking then. I am going!" That part won out. :-) As soon as I took the first few steps, I was glad. (*How often do we do the same in our work and leadership?*)

* I decided on the spur of the moment to go in a new direction, and discovered a path I've never been on before. It was a blessing. (*How can I reassure my people that the new paths God is leading us on hold unexpected blessings?*)

* I let my mind wander and simply paid attention to what was in front of me at the moment. How refreshing!

* A clear blue sky and bright sunshine sparkling on the snow at the path's edge.

* After about two minutes, the sound of birdsong began to surround me. (*How often have I missed out on that by staying cooped up and not getting out there where beauty and wonder and blessings are?*)

* I was amazed at how far I walked. I ended up on another side of town and saw things I never pay attention to. (*Simone Weil: Love is paying attention.*)

* On my way back I stopped on a bridge overlooking a clear rushing trout stream, and watched and listened to the water for some time. It was a beautiful reminder that the life force is unstoppable, that God is always creating something new, and that I am part of all of that.

* A hawk soared overhead.

* My decision to do one good thing for myself today — walk — led to another: to choose only healthy things to eat for lunch. (*Making one wise decision can open up other new possibilities and make other wise decisions easier.*)

*I feel better, inside and out!

Blessings of the *Vav*

My teacher Rabbi Shefa Gold has a chant: Renew within me a Spirit of Yes! from Psalm 51:12. I have a commitment to my soul's mission.

As a way of being kind and loving to myself, I am creating sustainability sisters and brothers to keep me on the path! LOL, admitting to myself that I need others, as together we can make anything happen. I will ask them to ask me the deep questions that will inspire me and keep me honest! And we will be sustaining each other.

Who are your sustainability partners?

7:52 AM

Tuesday, February 15, 2011

I Am Denouncing My Speed Queen Crown

After my first speeding ticket in four years — $129, ouch! — I have decided this is a sign I need to really look at my relationship with time.

In 1993, a Lakota medicine man in a one-on-one *I Ching* session told me something I have been grappling with ever since. The phrase is, "Make a friend of time." My immediate response to his words was to begin to cry, like I had been told some ultimate truth of the universe. I knew then that it was important, and yet I did not know how it related to my life. I think after all these years I may be getting to the core of this conundrum, this Zen *koan*.

As I drove home the 3 1/2 hours from St. Petersburg, I kept thinking what is it about time? What am I running from or toward that keeps me from being here? How have I not made a friend of time?

Then I remembered the sexual abuse I endured at age five that I hid from my consciousness until I was in my late 40s. And that dissociation is one way of running away from the pain of the moment. And that at 67 I no longer need to rush away from now, as I can take care of me, unlike during my childhood. And the power, skills, and personal best I feel behind the wheel, I can also feel in other places. I do not need to be behind the wheel of the car to do that!

Yet, this relationship with time is something else!

I remembered once following a woman who was driving so slowly I was about to bust a gasket! I needed to follow her, because she was leading me out of a development of homes to where I needed to go. I remembered being in awe of her steady driving, no rushing, no need to rush, she was sure and steady. I admired her driving and her groundedness to the earth. I wished I had that skill, and yet did not know if I ever could drive that slowly. What a paradox!!

So what has this to do with *and?* Well, the letter *vav* is a shape-shifter letter. In biblical Hebrew it is called a reversive *vav*, as it turns the past into the future and future into the present. In English, using the word *and* instead of *but* can change the possibilities and change the same-old thinking into a growth mindset. If we can hold more than one reality as true, we can change the world. Your pain and my pain are both awful and never should have happened, and they did.

So what do I get for denouncing my Speed Queen Crown? I get another chance at life. Just as the state police officer who stopped me gave me another chance by marking down the speed I was driving, so can I try something new. I will see what will happen not to rush through eating, the stop sign, the conversation, the uncomfortable moment. Maybe there is something I need to notice. Maybe I can learn to make a friend of time.

So why do you speed? What is your relationship to time? I need your help! Tell me your thoughts.

8:40 PM

Wednesday, February 16, 2011

HIT AND RUN

My sister-friend and I were having ones of those cross-the-bridge conversations, where I was bothered about something that had happened between us and I had asked to cross the bridge, as we learned in Hedy and Yumi's workshop, so we could talk to each other outside the distractions of our everyday life.

She had done something that left me going off by myself to take care of myself. My heart was walled up and defended, and underneath I was sad, angry, and feeling abandoned. And I was not going to tell that to anyone. I had learned a long time ago to shove all those feelings under the mat of the covering of my heart.

In our conversation, she was able to hear me and I was able to hear that she has a habit of hitting and running. In that moment, she is not in control of her feelings and instead of staying and talking about what she is feeling, she says what she needs to say and runs away. I could absolutely hear that — first, because I love her and want to stay in relationship with this long time sister-friend; and second, because I know I have done that same behavior.

Dissociation, running away from the now, is the other side of consciousness, says my therapist, Tim. As I move to being more awake in my life, I am choosing to run less and "be here now," to quote Ram Dass, the famous Harvard psychologist turned Hindu guru follower.

So, I ask myself what is so hard about being here? Can I notice my discomfort and breathe into it, as I do on the massage table when the spot touched is so painful and needs the oxygen to free the toxins, untie the knotted muscle?

Am I really wanting to free my soul from whatever covers her pureness, and to open the doors to possibilities when I stay present?

Do I want to admit my faith in something bigger than me, playing with me, keeping me hoping for love?

What are you thinking today about time, being conscious, love possibilities, and freedom?

⌨ **9:32 AM**

Thursday, February 17, 2011

TIIIIME IS ON MY SIDE, OH, YES IT IS!

I awoke singing the Rolling Stones' famous line.

I had been reading a story by a friend who responded to my request to help me make a friend of time. I am getting loads of help on this project, including my friends like Gila and Ginny, who wrote to me and filled in the gap of my knowledge by knowing it was the Stones' song I had floating in my head. Ginny even wrote that they first sang it on the *Ed Sullivan Show*! How many of you remember that show? LOL!

If I think of time as a friend, then there are no "dead" lines, just "do" dates. When I am "hooked in," as my astrologer friend, Dale O'Brien, says, then I am in the flow with the universe. Mystical Judaism tells of the transcendent soul being in alignment with the imminent soul, so the outside soul can drip its wisdom into the inside soul. That is called being in *mazal tov*! Right place, right time.

In my limited experience of consciousness, that state takes loads of self-trust, reflection, listening, breathing, stopping, laughing at myself, faith in something bigger than me, and a letting go of what I think is right by someone else's standard; being in integrity with me and the universe.

When I asked several friends if they had a story, Jean responded with this one:

I threw my brother, his wife, sons, and daughters-in-law out of my house some 13 years ago when he said something so violent to my partner and his sons. My partner and his sons were disturbed. I asked my brother about this and he said he did not know what they were talking about, and besides, I, his sister-host, used the wrong words. This response, I felt, was manipulative verbiage from a brother who went for his doctorate in semantic philosophy, on top of his wife criticizing the food I had prepared for Passover and stating that she hated being in my home, etc. I stated that I am valuable, my friends are valuable, and I will not tolerate that kind of verbal insult and ugliness. My brother and his wife laughed and made fun of me. I went to the door and ushered them all out with the comment that they are not welcome back into my home.

That did not stop me from calling them from time to time to stay connected, and know that someday we may fall back into another kind of rhythm. Literally a dozen years passed with me calling about twice a year, knowing that my brother is important to me and he will grow in his own time OR not, and I will be here when that happens. It happened and we are respectfully back in each other's lives with a few actual face-to-face encounters (at his home and in neutral territory). I have not invited them to my home yet and talked with them about them processing, in their way, the reactions they had to my home. I did not need to hear them; however, I do not want anymore facial and verbal negative reactions to me or my home. They need to determine when the time is right to reenter. I can wait because when the time is right, I will know, because I convulsed with agony at my decision to usher them out of my home.

I revisited the pain many times and was sure that I could live with whatever outcome, as I am so certain of nonattachment and attachment and impermanence, etc. In this case my reward is that we are again together, though there are moments that are a bit precarious. Noticing my behavior and response to a situation is important and I am OK with having violent, unwholesome reactions too. They do not last long, time is my friend, time is short, and I am OK with not practicing my belief 100 percent. It is another moment in time to keep learning and doing and redoing. PLUS I really do not want everything to be so calm. I think that is too boring; I like the various tonalities that come from me as an imperfect human being. AND I keep track of when enough is enough and that is TIME-based.

As I reread this story, I am preparing to facilitate a workshop on trust. My friend and colleague, Audrey, sent me an article by Stephen Covey on trust. He writes that, "Nothing is as fast as the speed of trust," at the personal and professional levels. I think how quickly we cover our hearts and how long it takes to uncover the heart and feel safe and build trust.

When I have *tiiiiime* on my side, being present to myself and the universe, then perhaps I am moving toward making a friend of time. If I weave my meditation practice into this equation, then when I notice without judging and stay with myself in all my emotions, thoughts, and visceral responses to the moment, then I am in *now* and my response is current and spot on!

Laughing at me, I leave you to continue the quest of learning about time by working at work responsibilities.

8:24 AM

Thursday, February 17, 2011

THE ONE DAY THAT IS DIFFERENT

Today is Friday, the one day I begin to slow down, breathe deeply, and take the time to connect with me, nature, family, and ritual. After lunch, I will clear off my table, take off the red tablecloth, and replace it with the white linen and lace cloth. Then I will put my candles into the crystal candleholders that Gila gave me when she moved from her Pittsburg home and place them with the wine cup that Ilise gave me for my ordination and embroidered Shabbat *challah* cloth that my friend Judith gave me to hold my bread. Judith's aunt had brought the *challah* cover from Germany. Then I will get the *tzedaka* box my mother gave me and the angel cards that were a gift from Rabbi Phyllis Berman when I worked with her at Elat Chayyim. When I can, I like the idea of starting my Sabbath on Friday afternoon, and bringing in the energy of all those who are not physically near me.

As I close a very busy and creative week, I wanted to offer some wisdom from my friends about time. I think each is important in its own ways.

I especially need to slow down and give attention to my daughters. Today my Facebook buddy and old friend Karen called to say her daughter is in the hospital in critical condition. At this moment I am forced again to remember how precious life is. And everything else does not really matter. For this Shabbat I will set some intentions that I hope I can keep, of making clear priorities around how I spend my time.

Syble, a colleague and friend from North Carolina, wrote in her daily Money Habitude blog, "When I was younger I expected things to be done in a timely way and promises related to deadlines were very important to me. Now, I automatically tack on days, weeks, months, and even years to a timeline. When a workman says he'll be here in three weeks, I assume if he makes it in six we're still 'on time.' When I'm starting a project that I think should take three to six months, I automatically think of at least a year. It's helped me avoid disappointment and frustration with delays. In the end, most of the time it really doesn't matter if it's today or not."

To be wise means to know that I only am aware of part of the story, and I must stay curious to keep receiving more.

A Florida friend wrote, "Several years ago, I one day just suddenly decided to start driving slowly, all the time. I now drive about 5 mph under the speed limit. I get almost everywhere almost as quickly as I did before and, more often than not, I meet cars that go flying by me at the next traffic light.

"I've had a checkered history with speeding tickets, including two in one day some years ago (one in my car and the other on my motorcycle, alas). When I was thoughtful about it, I chalked the habit up to a slowly simmering anxiety that I've always known I had. But I find that my newly adopted driving habit is probably the number one (maybe number two — running is right up there) thing I do to make peace with that anxiety.

"And the sequel to all this is that a couple of weeks ago I was driving down Military Trail at 40 mph and a blue sports car went zooming around me going at least 60, I'm sure. I found myself immediately getting an angry knot in the pit of my stomach. Then I stepped back from it and said to myself, 'Isn't that interesting? Maybe he has an emergency, or maybe he's late for an appointment, or maybe he too has an anxiety issue.' Whatever the reason, I clearly didn't have to let myself get sucked in by his behavior. And I didn't. Good example of a new slant on an old life lesson, I guess."

I love reading this and I laugh at how often I find myself aware of how the mind judges. When I am awake enough to notice this, I can choose joy. Other times, I add to my list of what is not right in the world. Then I begin to figure out how to be in the flow, to heal the seams that have cracked.

And the beat goes on and on and on! May your Sabbath and mine also have a taste of the world to come!

8:26 PM

Monday, February 21, 2011

Collecting Stories on Time

Today I heard Jim Croce's voice singing, "If I could put time in a bottle...." I am sure you know the rest. I have images of the bottle being the one you throw into the ocean with a message hoping for some Divine connection. Then I read Mahatma Gandhi's quote that there is more to life than increasing its speed, and I breathe deeply into this moment, wondering, "What is my relationship to speeding?"

What I think is interesting is my perspective on women in Judaism. There has always been a place for women associated with making a friend of time. More on this later.

In a coaching session the other day, one of my clients told me a story about time that she heard from an inspirational speaker. A taxi driver was trying to make as much money as he could, picking up fares, dropping them off, and looking for the next fare. One day he was sent to pick up a women and take her to hospice. It was her time to go, she said, and there was no one to say goodbye to.

Well, apparently, these words, this woman, her story touched the cab driver's heart. He began talking with her about her life, what had brought her to the city, where she had lived besides where he had picked her up. As she responded to his questions, he headed toward hospice, and made a decision that he was going to take his time and drive her around the city for her last tour. She was delighted with his attention.

The key teaching, I was told, is that the greatest gift you can give anyone is time. If you put yourself on the list, then you can also give yourself the gift of time. And attention is love, I have been told.

So, what have you been thinking about time? How do you spend your time? How do you give it away? What is your response to your generosity? How are you creative with time?

Barry Oshry, president of Power + Systems, created a workshop simulation in which the facilitators call a TOOT, a "time out of time" during the three-hour workshop process. During this 20-minute TOOT people are asked to stop, reflect, and share their experiences with one another. Then the simulation begins again.

How often do I do that? Probably not enough. Now that I have thought about it, maybe I will do it more. I learned from Bill Drath, adjunct faculty at the Center for Creative Leadership, that a key component of action learning is to "stop, reflect, write" to keep people in the learning mindset.

Maybe today I will take some time to give myself attention by stopping, reflecting, breathing, and listening to my heart, my body, my mind — and then laugh with joy at being with me!

And I have noticed that since I have been focusing on time, I have been slowing my driving down, just a bit.

1:43 PM

Sunday, June 5, 2011

What Keeps Me from Being an Effective Leader?

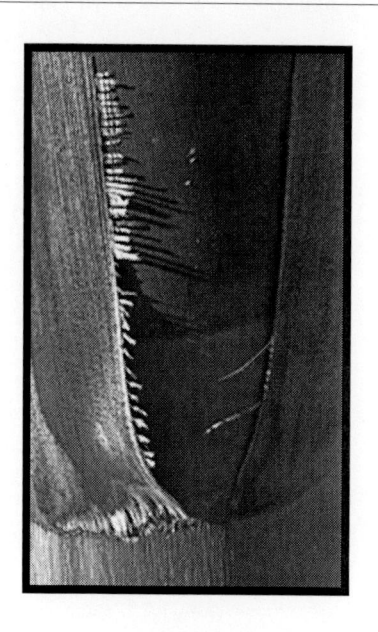

Palm tree unfolding

In our training yesterday we asked the group, "What keeps me from being an effective leader?"

Reflecting this morning on yesterday's events, I thought that one of those elements is my self-doubt — having to prove myself to myself — that being a white, Jewish, lesbian woman keeps me from being all I can be in the world.

I am in Jamaica, where I am a minority in terms of the color of my skin. Yesterday, a man I am working with told me that when he first saw me he thought I was a racist. Over the day I proved to him that I am a kind person and that his initial reaction to me was incorrect.

I was blown away by his disclosure and honored that he felt safe enough to say what was in his head and heart to me. I was delighted the cat was out of the bag. The topic often not talked about was put on the table: racism. Of course I am a racist in my own way. We all use various reasons to build walls to keep our self emotionally and sometimes physically and psychically safe, and to keep people out. I am learning to mange these fears and open my heart to the truth: We are all one.

There is a part of me that knows in a past life I was an African slave living in the Low Country of South Carolina. When the Jamaican man told me he saw my soul, not the color of my skin, I thought *Halleluya*!!!! Sweet Jesus, I am home! He sees my soul, not the color of my skin, that outer covering that can hide the true self from others so I am not recognized!

I am being seen for who I truly am. He not only got me, he merged with me, the color of my skin no longer separated us.

What a great question to ask again and again and again!! What makes me an effective leader?

Each asking allows me to be open to new perspectives. The blessing of *and* is a softening of boundaries around the end of thoughts. I can give myself permission to continue the conversation, over and over again. I am learning from a new perspective what it means to never give up; to trust that there is another corner to walk round, and I may never see that corner until I say *and*.

I am a *Vav-nik*, I believe in the possibilities of healing, of opportunities dreamed of and yet not found — YET! I am laughing out loud at myself and this life and the gifts that come every day, even when I do not expect them. I am choosing life, having lived through the moments of blessings and curses. I am Home!

2:05 PM

Sunday, June 26, 2011

Personal Best

Dessert, Israel

Do you ever wonder, looking at desserts, if any of them think, "I am better than that one next to me because of my color"? Or, "Will they pick me first because I am bigger"? Or, "No one will pick me because I don't have any fruit"?

Several years ago I saw a movie, *Personal Best*, about two women athletes who fell in love while competing for the love and attention of each other and a man. For me it was both a beautiful and a painful movie. The phrase *personal best*, the title of the film, has remained with me and has helped me deal with the mind's default of competition and envy and doubt.

I am making a public commitment and taking a vow, like I did at Plum Village so many years ago, when I took on the five mindfulness precepts of the Order of Interbeing. Now, I am choosing to notice when I am in those narrow-martyr-victim-slave places, and I am going to choose to think *personal best* whenever the mind puts me in competition with, or feeling less or more than, anyone else.

I am amazing, I am unique, I am like no one else. And I have a part to play no one else can, or is going to play! My unique matter makes a difference even when I think it does not!

So why bother! Even in my driving, I am going to laugh at myself when I race down the road to beat someone else, or hear, "What will they think?" As long as I choose to treat myself as if I were my own lover, with kindness and compassion, I am in the right place and right time. Doing my best to be me, including me on the list of people I care about!

I am going to have fun, choose joy, and laugh at myself. That is my choice to help mend the tears in the universe! I am going to engage in what Chuck and David, my buddies and colleagues at the Center for Creative Leadership, call "serious play" in their book, *The Leader's Edge: Six Creative Competencies for Navigating Complex Challenges*.

Serious, because I am focused on my intention to learn to live with myself with deep compassion as an image of the Divine.

Play, because I love to play, have fun, be joyful, for I know that is the best space for me to learn, as I am open and curious and willing to be vulnerable and make mistakes.

Blessings on your path of being your *personal best*; and may we meet on the road and smile at each other's comings and goings, as we place a hand on our heart, nod, and say, "Namaste." I do see the G!D in you as you see the G!D in me.

7:37 PM

Monday, July 4, 2011

The Wall Is Down: The Heart Is Receiving in This Moment

Road Leading to the Heart

I am leaving the place where I have lived for four years, and now it is safe to let those I have met into my heart. I laugh at noticing my patterns.

I am moving on to try again to find Home. Not that I did not find pieces of it here. Wonderful people, as long as I kept them at a distance, and a warm tropical climate that provided me plenty of opportunities to grow. I learned how to sail, what it was like to display some art work publicly, and vacation with the snorkel club I had just met. I even committed to six months of teaching and kept my promise, and learned so much about connecting with six amazing women and Judaism and mindfulness and meditation. I owned my own home for the first time and then sold it at a loss! That was an interesting moment to rationalize away!!

My father died and then my mother was killed and now I am an orphan. What I thought I was moving here for no longer exists. Then I needed to think where in the world do I want to live, now that the roots that grew me have shriveled up.

You never really know why you move someplace until after you leave, so I have another few weeks to figure that out. I am beginning to experience what it means to love and to be loved and be able to receive that love. This is real cool! Shivering cool, sometimes!! LOL!!

I am taking the time to really experience the loss of leaving this place that harbored me and the amazing women and men I have met. I am noticing the sadness and grief I am experiencing, and the caring I feel for those I am leaving, and will never have the same casual and purposeful relationship with. I even let the mind wonder why I am leaving these people I have finally opened my heart to. I know it is only in the leaving that I have the perspective to see how welcomed I have been. And I am grateful for this place of seeing and the heart that is receiving, even at a distance.

Too late, I am reminded, the condo is sold, the boxes are being packed, and a new physical space is awaiting me — as is my next opportunity to open my heart and not wait for them to open theirs. Maybe I will do it differently this time. Maybe these wonderful people who await me know me so well and love me so much that I can walk in with an open heart. Maybe I will go there ready to receive their attention and appreciation for who I am, this amazing woman doing her personal best.

And yes, it is true, things are changing all the time and there is always another opportunity to face the fear and manage the delicate balance between connected and separate, the circle and line dance. **4:28 PM**

Monday, July 22, 2011

STANDING ON THE THRESHOLD

TZiPi in Cuzco, Peru

Standing at the doorway to the unknown, I may appear full of joy, yet this casual pose may not tell the whole story.

I sat in my bathroom the other day, looking around and appreciating the natural light that flows through the large window, the broad counter that gives room for many items, and the long the bathtub that I have so enjoyed luxuriating and soaking in, to the point of moving into dreamland. And I think, I am going to miss what this room offers. I am appreciating the other gifts this home has offered, hardwood floors, lots of light, great energy, lots of room to move around on this first floor, the opportunity to meet the most amazing people, and to invite these people into my home to enjoy what I love!

I know this is good to love where I am leaving, and to be able to know why I am moving on. I read somewhere that it is best to leave what you love.

So I am feeling sad about leaving and I am excited about what awaits me in my next home that I will make my own, too! There is light, there is water, there is an upstairs and a downstairs, and there is my family, who is thrilled I am choosing to live close to them!

I stand on this threshold, I remember my ancestors, the boundary crossers, who teach us, remember Me-Us-We, you are never alone, you are loved always eternally. And I am grateful to follow in their path, the wandering Jews, who occasionally build nests to grow within.

11:37 AM

Wednesday, August 17, 2011

Disorientation and the Antidote

Unfurling fern

I am having lunch looking out at the gorgeous blue sky and wide expanse of water dotted with white boats.

My eyes wisp by my car, also outside my window, and something is not right. The color on the back of the car has changed. Then I remember my new license plate! And I wake up and laugh!

So many things like that are happening as I adjust mentally and emotionally to my new space, town, and culture. So many things to learn. So much to understand to be emotionally safe here, and feel as if I am a contributing member to my chosen community. Funny how important it is for me to give.

I think about automatic thinking and mindfulness, and how I live my life depending on things being the same. Like a blind person who learns their space and gets thrown off balance when things change. Am I that blind woman, yearning for the familiar? *Yes, and*....

I am a teacher and practitioner of improvisation, mindfulness practice, compassion, and loving-kindness. I laugh as I am still learning. I am not ready to catch the wave!

And the enlightenment I yearn for? It happens in moments only! I smile at my settling with this knowing.

I notice how interdependent I am on everything that happens to keep me awake. Soon I will be blowing my *shofar* every day to remind me to wake up and come home to my true self. Some days the *shofar* will be just another experience to add to all the others, like the change in color of my license plate, to keep me awake as I walk the path, laughing at the gifts that welcome me home. And I do not have to do anything except keep walking and staying awake.

Deep breath!!!

2:41 PM

Sunday, August 21, 2011

Circumcise Your Heart and Do Not Have Such a Stiff Neck

Wounded Heart Being Touched by Many Hearts

Will you help me practice the uncovering of my heart so I can consciously know, be viscerally aware, that I am receiving unconditional love from the *ma'ayan raz*, eternal spring?

Will you be my mirror and my partner to support me in experiencing that I am safe in this world to receive the universal love that is available? I want to face the fears that keep my heart protected and begin to know what it feels like to feel worthy of receiving unconditional love, without strings. I have felt moments of this love, as during my ordination, an expansive, glorious, sweet, adoring love. I also feel deep love of and connectedness with my daughters. I also want to receive their love.

In meditation this morning, in following the circular movement of the mind from Here to there and back to Here, I experienced an awareness of how covered I keep my heart. And that the phrase from the Torah that I have had a strong relationship with, "circumcise your heart and don't have a stiff neck," was a message to me personally. I began to cry, deep sobs of awareness.

I know now that I learned an internal stance in childhood to lean over, hunch my shoulders, keep my head down, my hands over the chest and groin, and lean forward into the wind. That was the only way I could move with people and be safe, keep my heart protected, and exist until I could become aware of other ways of being; to live my life fully open, head up, shoulders back, chest exposed to the elements, knowing I could take very good care of myself and that I am lovable and safe. And I could create sacred space where I would engage in crucial conversations and learn about me within a relationship.

I am no longer willing to use my energy to keep my heart covered. I have other things to do with that energy. I feel expressive and I am no longer tongue-tied.

Will you play with me? Will you be my partner and be open to love, unconditional love that speaks from the heart-mind, body-spirit, that engages all of me in a compassionate and kind manner, creating sacred space to allow us both to be Present?

Are you ready for me? Am I ready for me to be out and naked and fully alive in the world? Can there be three amazing women in one family? YES!!!! *and....* LOL!!!!

I must uncover this heart and be open to change, for if I do not, You will do the uncovering for me! And that is what I read in the Holy Scriptures.

11:45 AM

Monday, August 29, 2011

Practicing
Surrender

Banyan trees, West Palm Beach, FL

I went on a work and play road trip to NC this last week, driving from Beaufort, SC, to Greensboro to Asheville and Brevard, NC, then back home. I drove blind. You read correctly. I turned on my GPS and prayed.

I did not look at the map that sat in my glove compartment. I did not have my Google Maps printout, nor did I call anyone on the phone and ask them to guide me. I set the Nuvi and prayed and took direction. Because I was the only one in the car, I could not look too often, as I had agreed to not look at it while driving.

I get chills up my spine when I think about how brave I was to let go of my deeeeep need to be fiercely independent and follow the legacy of my parents. I thought often, why am I doing this? I like seeing the whole picture. I adore knowing where I am going! Do I need another gadget? And knowing those are the words of a woman who does not like change and who wants to be practical!

I was also hearing Ilana's voice in my head, asking why I won't let anyone help me. And the other voice of mine asking what kind of role model am I to my daughter. Do I want her to build walls of, "I can do it myself, thank you," too!?

This is a big one! Letting go is soooo hard! And neuroscientists' exploration of how G!D affects the brain found that faith was the number one influence to neuro-plasticity, embracing the unknown.

It is good practice, this surrendering. And it is only to a machine. I am practicing learning how to live near family in my new home, learning I am not alone, learning about being connected, and learning how to JUST receive the love of others.

I must admit I am slow extending the net to practice believing in the unconditional love of my G!D. I am learning this too, and that I also can learn to love me, even after all these years, with the help of learning to take down the walls and experience the love given.

So thanks, dear friend Ruthie, for encouraging me to buy my first GPS, and my Gaelic friend Ginny for helping me practice receiving love from my *anam cara*, "soul friend." And to everyone else who has been patient with this heart and still wants me in their life.

Elul begins tomorrow night. The 30 days of blowing the *shofar* to wake my soul up and bring me back to my true self commences at sundown. Thirty days of practicing and learning, so on the anniversary of the beginning of the world, the next new moon, I will be ready to forgive myself for all the moments when

I doubted my lovableness, and invite me back into my heart and celebrate the beginning of the Rosh Hashana, the new year, 5772.

I am learning to believe in the concept of a learning community, and that I am smart enough to learn while living within the boundaries of this physical reality. I must be loved! LOL!! Why else would I do this!!

7:14 AM

Friday, September 2, 2011

Learning to Play on the Offensive Team

Koh Samui, Surat Thani Province, Thailand

So, you must be curious and wondering what offensive team? The team that has the ball and calls the plays and goes for the goal, of course!

The agile ones, the light-on-their feet ones! Not the ones who offend!! LOL!!

Well, I might have to offend some people on my way down the field! And that is what happens when you are focused on your soul's journey, making meaning of your life. Some people will be sleeping and not want to be bothered. Some people will like you just the way you are, so they do not have to change. And, as one of my favorite poets, Mary Oliver, wrote, sometimes you have to walk away from those voices and save the only life you can — yours. There are others you will join on your journey.

Phyllis came to visit for a few days. Whenever a Baba Lover who is also from Boston, an Aries, lives alone, and is very brilliant, gets together with another Jewish, Boston-born, Aries who lives alone and likes to please, after a few days sparks fly! Divine sparks that want to be redeemed, so the soul can be uncovered. In the unsettling chaos, Phyllis spoke a truth: "Be offensive!"

She had seen me become defensive and in her inimitable style had told me what to do, instead of what not to do. Apologizing for her directness, she said the words again, "Be offensive."

After brushing off my ego and settling down to hear what she had to say, I pondered her words. Offensive? What does that mean?

What do I need to be on that team? In shape and focused, have clear intentions, be a team player and flexible, improvisational, transformational, and love the game! And maybe I have to learn it is OK to offend, say it like it is, the truth as I see it! Oy vey!! Well, I tell myself, everyone, including me, needs a clear mirror. Like the 360s we use to help leaders get their effect on their world. This intention is a great one to set for Elul. While I am learning about loving You as You love me, I will hold on to the balance of love and power: soul work and connectedness to others. I get a shiver down my spine knowing this truth will shed a few pounds and get me closer to the truth: My G!D is everywhere.

1:35 PM

Saturday, September 3, 2011

A Taste of the World to Come

Plant, Peru

Blessings of Being Awake

Shabbat shalom, blessings of a restful day full of moments of a taste of the world to come, I wish to you and to me. And I ponder the days that led up to this day.

This week in Beaufort two young men died. One took his own life and one died as a result of an accident. Both, I pray, have souls who are at peace. Both left families and friends grieving, wondering if they could have done something differently and feeling sorrow and yearning for one more day with their friend, son, brother, lover, husband, father.

I never met either and I have heard stories from my daughter, as my grandson struggles to understand this death of a friend and peer.

This week a dear friend struggled with depression. Her mind imagined a future without hope for a freedom — a reprieve in her life — that, in her past, she rarely experienced and deeply yearned for.

This week my adopted grandson told his father and his stepmother he is not returning to college. He will be leaving for California to seek work and a break from the routine of the last five years.

This week I met several new people who hold possibilities of a good life for me here in the marshes and waters of the Low Country. Some kind and good women and men who live outside the box of societal norms and expectations. This week a new friend changed my perspective of myself by offering herself through deep conversations.

This week my daughter showed me her joy at having me physically closer to her.

This week I began seeing and experiencing the patterns of the Presence of the Divine in my life. I began getting the message that I have really and truly never been alone! I began to see, as Jacob was said to have spoken, God was in this place and I, i did not know.

Spiritual Practice

With this seeing and knowing, I have set an intention to continue to meditate, chant with my shruti box, pull my Mother Peace Cards, consult and study with others who know differently than I so I can expand my perspective. I remain in a place of not knowing, so I can be surprised with the joy of possibilities. I can laugh like Sarah was reported to have done, when she was told she would be a mother at 99. And perhaps, I too, like my role model and matriarch, will birth something when I think I am dried up and barren. Or maybe I will notice the amazing lives I have touched, and get to walk with — and that will be enough!!!

Society of the *Vav*, *Vav-nik* Intention

As I stand at the threshold of the next moment, I will use my head and my heart, as I shatter the still energy, moving forward over the threshold into the next moment. I do make a difference. This is justice. This is transformation.

10:50 AM

Tuesday, September 6, 2011

HOLY UNION, HIEROS GAMOS

Plant, Peru

I want to enter and be entered
I yearn to know what it feels like
To have G!D within me
While being able to enjoy
The deliciousness of
Being Present with You

I want to breathe in *Ruach HaKodesh*, the Holy Spirit
And then breathe back into You
Renewing myself as the moon
Renews each month

I am made in the image of *HaShem*, the One Without End
Loving women and loving men
Just like She does
Why deny the fact that
My heart is as large as His

I am Ariadne and I am *Shechina*, the Indwelling Presence of the Divine
I am Sarah, princess of the world
I evolve and transform with each breath
I am love and I am hate
I am Hagar, the stranger within me
Yearning to be known

I am an individual, unique as the moment
I am Abraham, confused in love
I am never the enemy, only Darkness
From which Light can come

Come closer, My Dear
Let us be known to each other
So we can laugh and cry together
We can mourn and celebrate our lives
Lived and soon to be born

8:26 AM

Sunday, September 11, 2011

I Had a Dream

Flora growing from cracks in stone wall

I had a dream this morning before I awoke and I was full of joy and love when I opened my eyes. I am not sure what the dream was all about; I am choosing not to analyze, and I am not going to review it here. I am going to write it down and savor the feelings, people, colors, conversations.

Then I am going to notice how my life enfolds.

I had a moment of awareness and enlightenment yesterday as I readied for bed. When I am on retreat, I am mindful of the present moment, slow in movement, noticing how I lift my foot, place a plate down on the table, choose my food, and more! I am taking time to be with me, focusing on now, coming back to this moment when the mind begins to do its dance of: "Look at what he is doing," "How about that thought?" "Can you believe what she did?" or, "Ooh, that smells good and I am so hungry."

I have been telling people about some of my experiences on various retreats and how much I enjoyed them. I began to wonder, "Why only then?"

As I moved the plants on my stoop, I shoved the hand-painted ceramic pot that held a miniature snake plant into the railing and one arm cracked and fell into the bushes. I was shocked; I thought I was being so careful. Everything had been going so well, the storm door was off, and I had hung a screen door, with the help of my neighbor Dale, to let in the fresh air. I thought I was careful; apparently not enough!

Then I remembered impermanence and loss are just emotions we tag to an experience.

The mind wandered and I remember supporting others on their silent retreat at Elat Chayyim, offering them water as they worked in the hot kitchen. I loved serving and caring for those choosing silence — or on all the retreats, the many experiences and learning. In Thailand with Rosemary and Steve, I learned that silence is not a punishment and I was never alone. In Pondicherry, India, at the Sri Aurobindo Ashram, I learned I am deeply connected to the spiritual world through my body. I stayed there long enough to hear the Mother, one of the spiritual leaders of the ashram, now deceased, speak to me on the rooftop of one of the guesthouses, on the anniversary of her birthday: "Yea, thou you walk through the valley of the shadow of death, I am with you." In Israel on a silent retreat weekend and again while living at Plum Village in France with Thich Nhat Hanh, I learned about the power of discipline, focus, and faith, and to go back to my roots. At the Insight Meditation Society, a *vipassana* Buddhist retreat center in Barre, MA, I discovered how unsafe I felt in the world as a Jew. And on a two-week silent retreat, I wanted Hebrew wisdom to balance the Buddhism that was being taught. I asked Sylvia Boorstein, one of the teachers, for help during the *metta*, loving-kindness retreat, and she offered me what I now know as the Priestly Blessing in Hebrew.

And how can I forget Stephen Levine and the very first silent retreat I ever experienced? He responded to a letter I had written him that I must learn that I am my own teacher and I must learn to trust myself, trust the process, and treasure myself. Treasure myself — what a concept — I continue to learn what it means, along with love myself and make a friend of time.

I laugh out loud as I awaken to my life and put the pieces together, making a collage of extraordinary beauty, as stunning as my daughter Andrea's quilts.

8:17 AM

Wednesday, September 28, 2011

Closure

Fall leaves, Salem, MA

Before there can be a beginning, there must be an end.

This morning I pulled the Death card from my Motherpeace deck. This is the last day of 5771, I remind myself as I read what Vicki Noble writes: This is not about a physical death, only a metaphor for some experience of dying and rebirth.

I had just decided to write an entry in my blog. And when I began the title section, I could only think that this is an ending of four years of writing in this blog. I have, with the encouragement of Tim, my beloved Buddhist therapist, begun creating a book of the last four years' musings. I have been imagining reading from the completed book to my students of mindfulness-meditation. So it will happen, after I learn about self-publishing through the help of the Internet site, Blub. I sit with tears coming down my face. How do I say goodbye to this ritual of writing the Society of the *Vav*? How do I end this love affair I have had with the Hebrew letter *vav*? I do not want to say goodbye, *adieu, ciao*! For that would leave emptiness. And G!D forbid I should feel that bottomless pit of emptiness!!

How do I know it is over? Where will I go? Who will I be if I am not a *Vav-nik*? Or will I be that forever, whether I write or not? So many questions, so few answers. Letting go is a powerful exercise for me in this moment.

I ask myself, "What would the *vav* say?" And I hear, "Once a connection is made, it is never severed." I am a *Vav-nik* forever, and I am learning what it means to be connected with family, friends, nature; to trust this connection and to trust me even more to know I can take care of myself. I am amazing and there is work left to do that is all mine, along with others. I am on a mission to heal the world, one heart at a time. I am learning my skills and refining them as I move through the River of Light.

The first entry of the Society of the *Vav* was on listening. I am continuing to learn how to listen. I am learning what it means to listen to the inner voice, the G!D within me. She is so wise. Like the character in Ntozake Shange's *For Colored Girls Who Have Considered Suicide / When the Rainbow Is Enuf*, I am owning that G!D is within me. The Indwelling Divine Spirit, *Shechina*, She dwells within. I need to listen to the still voice, not just the loud ones that say, "You are going for a trip around the world" or "I want to be a rabbi." The more subtle ones that demand I be quiet and be still, to slow down so the wind does not distort the sounds and words coming through me to me. That is being kind to myself, treating myself as if I were my own lover. I am a lifelong learner, thank G!D!

Otherwise I would be up a creek without a paddle!! LOL!!
So this is how I will leave you, with an end, a celebration of what has come and an *and*...
And, of course, a blessing:
As I watched the sun set on this last day of 5771, I mused on how grateful I am for your Presence in my life
and I wondered
am I ready for this Rosh Hashana and what she will bring?
Not that it matters, she is going to come anyway,
and I, i am going to welcome Her with open arms and an open heart!

Who would turn away sweetness and joy?

Shana tova u'mituka, tikateivu v'tikateimu!
May this year be good and sweet
and may you and all you hold dear be written and sealed in the Book of Life for yet another year!

And if that does not happen, may we come together to support each other through the narrow spaces,
knowing Love is always there to comfort. And we are love!

Blessings of joy and sweetness, health and love in 5772!

9:00 AM

Agudat HaVav
The Society of the *Vav*

The mission of the Society of the *Vav* is to generate thought, conversation, and practice around the idea of inclusiveness. The energy intelligence of the *vav*, sixth letter of the Hebrew alphabet, is eternal connection and supports the idea that the mind is able to hold multiple realities, each as truth, none being better than the other. For example, there is no hierarchy of pain or joy.

And with the practice of mindfulness, a visceral energy shift can be experienced when the word *and* is used instead of *but*. This experience can help us to perceive the dynamic flow of life. There are no stops, no negations, only pauses in the river of our life — one experience collaborating with another, creating a dynamic collage.

The Society of the *Vav* supports the idea that life is improvisational and we are continually learning to dance with the needs of the moment, building bridges between people and things and, on a deeper level, emotions and heart-mind thoughts and behaviors.

And that the mind's suffering is being comforted and transformed as we learn to honor a paradoxical state of being-ness, never settling for either-or thinking. We are separate, unique entities and we are One, divinely interconnected. And our individuality is the unique gift we each bring to our leadership in making the world a better place.

AGUDAT HAVAV
THE SOCIETY OF THE VAV

Giving attention to the linking energy-intelligence of the sixth Hebrew letter — *vav* — and its meaning of *and* that will save the world.

With great honor inducts as an honorary member

Who is Intentionally Redeeming a Spark of Hebrew Wisdom and

is a *Vav-nik*.

A *Vav-nik* has committed to living a unique paradoxical life of connection, transformation, and integration in intent and behavior; for this knowing allows for expression of all thoughts and emotions, and one can only rise to one's highest good, constantly birthing and unearthing universal truths that heal the pain and the illusion of separation, making the world a better place.

We are blessed to have been nurtured, sustained, and brought to this moment in time. *Halleluya!*

Bibliography

Arnst, William, and Betsy Chasse. *What the Bleep Do We Know.* DVD. Lord of the Wind Films, 2004.

Beattie, Melody. *Journey to the Heart: Daily Meditations on the Path to Freeing Your Soul.* New York: HarperOne, 1996.

Bodaken, Bruce, and Robert Fritz. *The Managerial Moment of Truth: The Essential Step in Helping People Improve Performance.* New York: Free Press, 2011.

Brown, Juanita, and David Isaacs. *The World Café: Shaping Our Futures Through Conversations That Matter.* San Francisco: Bernett-Kohler Publishers, 2005.

Buber, Martin. *I and Thou.* New York: Scribner, 2000.

Cameron, James. *Avatar.* DVD. Twentieth Century Fox, 2009.

Cameron, Julia. *The Artist's Way.* New York: Jeremy P. Tarcher/Putnam, 1992.

Chaleff, Ira. *Courageous Followers: Standing Up to & for Our Leaders*, third edition. Williston, VT: Berrett-Koehler Publishers, 2009.

Coelho, Paulo, and Alan R. Clarke. *The Alchemist, anniversary edition.* New York: HarperCollins, 2006.

Cooperrider, David L., and Diana Whitney. *Appreciative Inquiry: A Positive Revolution in Change.* Williston, VT: Berrett-Koehler Publishers, 2005.

Coppola, Sofia. *Lost in Translation.* American Zoetrope Tohokushinsha Film, 2003.

Covey, Steven M.R., and Rebecca R. Merrill. *The Speed of Trust: The One Thing That Changes Everything.* Tampa, FL: Free Press, 2008.

Croce, Jim. "Time in a Bottle." Produced by Terry Cashman, ABC, 1972.

Dass, Ram. *Be Here Now.* San Cristobal, NM: Lama Foundation, 1971.

Dobkin, Alix. *My Red Blood: A Memoir of Growing Up Communist, Coming Onto the Greenwich Village Folk Scene, and Coming Out in the Feminist Movement.* Boston, MA: Alyson Books, 2009.

Drinkwater, Gregg, Joshua Lesser, and David Shneer, editors. *Torah Queeries: Weekly Commentaries on the Hebrew Bible*. New York: New York University Press, 2009.

Dweck, Carol. *Mindset: The New Psychology of Success*. New York: Ballantine Books, 2007.

Epstein, Mark. *Thoughts Without a Thinker: Psychotherapy from a Buddhist Perspective*. New York: Basic Books, 1995.

Ernst, Chris, and Donna Chrobot-Mason. *Boundary Spanning Leadership: Six Practices for Solving Problems, Driving Innovation, and Transforming Organizations*. McGraw-Hill, 2010.

Friedman, Debbie. "Not by Might, Not by Power," 1974.

Friedman, Thomas L. *The World is Flat: A Brief History of the Twenty-first Century*. Farrar, Straus and Giroux, 2005.

Gafni, Marc. *Soul Prints: Your Path to Fulfillment*. New York: Fireside, 2001.

Gafni, Marc. Comments made during Maggid Training course at Elat Chayyim, Accord, NY, 2005.

Gibran, Kahlil. *The Prophet*. New York: Alfred A. Knopf, 1923.

Gilbert, Elizabeth. *Eat, Pray, Love: One Woman's Search for Everything Across Italy, India and Indonesia*. New York: Penguin Books, 2007.

Gold, Shefa. *Torah Journeys: The Inner Path to the Promised Land*. Teaneck, NJ: Ben Yehuda Press, 2006.

Goldberg, Natalie. *Writing Down the Bones: Freeing the Writer Within*. Boston, MA. Shambhala Publications, 1986.

Goldsmith, Marshall, and Shane Clester. *What Got You Here Won't Get You There: A Round Table Comic: How Successful People Become Even More Successful*. Mundeen, IL: Round Table Companies, 2011.

Hanh, Thich Naht. *Interbeing: Fourteen Guidelines for Engaged Buddhism*. Parallax Press, 1987.

Haralick, Robert M. *The Inner Meaning of the Hebrew Letters*. Northvale, NJ: Jason Aronson, 1995.

Harvey, Andrew. *Hidden Journey: A Spiritual Awakening*. Penguin Books, 1992.

Hendrix, Harville. *Keeping the Love You Find: A Personal Guide*. New York: Pocket Books, 1992.

Henley, William Ernest. "Invictus." *Book of Verses*, 1875.

Heschel, Abraham Joshua. *The Sabbath*. Farrar, Straus and Giroux, 1951.

Hicks, Esther, and Jerry Hicks. *The Law of Attraction: The Basics of the Teachings of Abraham*. Carlsbad, CA: Hay House, 2006.

Hoffman, Edward. *The Hebrew Alphabet: A Mystical Journey*. San Francisco, CA: Chronicle Books, 1998.

Horth, David M., and Charles J Palus. *The Leader's Edge: Six Creative Competencies for Navigating Complex Challenges*. New York: Jossey-Bass, 2002.

Idliby, Ranya, Suzanne Oliver, and Priscilla Warner. *The Faith Club: A Muslim, A Christian, A Jew — Three Women Search for Understanding*. New York: Free Press, 2007.

Kabat-Zinn, Jon. *Coming to Our Senses: Healing Ourselves and the World Through Mindfulness*. New York: Hyperion Books, 2005.

Kahane, Adam. *Power and Love: A Theory and Practice of Social Change*. San Francisco: Berrett-Koehler Publishers, 2010.

Kaplan, Aryeh. *Meditation and the Bible*. Red Wheel/Weiser, 1978.

Kaplan, Aryeh. *Jewish Meditation: A Practical Guide*. New York: Schocken Books, 1985.

Katie, Byron, and Stephen Mitchell. *Loving What Is: Four Questions That Can Change Your Life*. New York: Three Rivers Press, 2003.

Kavanaugh, James J. *There are Men too Gentle to Live Among Wolves*. Steven J. Nash Publishers, 1991.

Kegan, Robert, and Lisa Laskow Lahey. *How the Way We Talk Can Change the Way We Work: Seven languages for Transformation*. Jossey-Bass, 2002.

King, Martin Luther, Jr. *Where Do We Go from Here?* in *A Call to Conscience: The Lanmark Speeches of Dr. Martin Luther King, Jr.*, edited by Clayborne Carson and Kris Shepherd. New York: Grand Central Publishing, 2002.

Kushner, Lawrence. *Book of Letters: A Mystical Hebrew Alphabet*. Woodstock, VT: Jewish Lights Publishing, 1991.

Leading Across Boundaries, Phase III: Action Learning Leadership Projects. Greensboro, NC: Center for Creative Leadership, 2011.

Lennon, John, and Paul McCartney. "All You Need is Love." Produced by George Martin, Parlophone, 1967.

Levine, Ondrea. *The Healing I Took Birth For: An Autobiography of Ondrea Levine*. Aperion Books, 2012.

Levine, Stephen. *Healing into Life and Death*. New York: Anchor Books, 1989.

Lewis, Hal. M. *From Sanctuary to Boardroom: A Jewish Approach to Leadership*. Lanham, MD: Rowman & Littlefield Publishers, 2006.

Lorde, Audre. *Zami: A New Spelling of My Name*. Freedom, CA: Crossing Press, 1982.

Madson, Patricia Ryan. *Improv Wisdom: Don't Prepare, Just Show Up*. New York: Bell Tower, 2005.

Martin, Roger L. *The Opposable Mind: Winning Through Integrative Thinking*. Harvard Business School Press, 2007.

Michaelson, Jay. *Everything is God: The Radical Path of Nondual Judaism*. Trumpeter, 2009.

Moorhouse, Jocelyn, and P.J. Hogan. *Unconditional Love*. DVD. New Line Cinema, 2002.

Morinis, Alan. *Everyday Holiness: The Jewish Spiritual Path of Mussar*. Boston, MA: Trumpeter, 2008.

Munk, Michael L. *The Wisdom in the Hebrew Alphabet*. Brooklyn, NY: Mesorah Publications, 1986.

Newberg, Andrew, and Mark Robert Waldman. *How God Changes Your Brain: Breakthrough Findings from a Leading Neuroscientist*. New York: Ballantine Books, 2010.

Noble, Vicki. *Motherpeace: A Way to the Goddess through Myth, Art, and Tarot*. New York: HarperCollins, 1983.

Novogratz, Jacqueline. *The Blue Sweater: Bridging the Gap Between Rich and Poor in an Interconnected World.* New York, NY: Rodale Books, 2009.

O'Donohue, John. *Anam Cara: A Book of Celtic Wisdom.* New York: Harper Collins, 1998.

Oliver, Mary. *New and Selected Poems, Volume One.* Boston: Beacon Press, 1992.

Oshry, Barry. *Seeing Systems: Unlocking the Mysteries of Organizational Life.* New York, NY: Berrett-Koehler, 2007.

Ott-Toltz, Phyllis, and Barbara Bamberger Scott. *Love Bade Me Welcome.* Lake Forest, CA: Behler Publications, 2006.

Palus, Chuck J., and David M. Horth. *Visual Explorer Playing Card Set.* Greensboro, NC: CCL Press, 2010.

Parashar, Avish. *Say "Yes, And!": 2 Little Words That Will Transform Your Career, Organization, and Life!* Lexington, KY: Avish Parashar Productions, 2012.

Patel, Eboo. *Acts of Faith: The Story of an American Muslim, the Struggle for the Soul of a Generation.* Boston: Beacon Press, 2007.

Radonsky, TZiPi. *Text Mapping the Erotic Life of Sarah: Woman, Matriarch, Primary Female Source of Hebrew Wisdom.* Manuscript completed for rabbinical ordination requirements, 2005.

Radonsky, Vivien E. *Factors Influencing Lesbians' Direct Disclosure of Their Sexual Orientation.* Ann Arbor, MI: U.M.I. Dissertation Services, 1993.

Ragovoy, Jerry. "Time Is On My Side," performed by The Rolling Stones. Produced by Andrew Loog Oldham, 1964.

Ribner, Mindy. *Kabbalah Month by Month: A Year of Spiritual Practice and Personal Transformation.* New York: Jossey-Bass, 2002.

Riso, Don Richard, and Russ Hudson. *The Wisdom of the Enneagram: The Complete Guide to the Psychological and Spiritual Growth for the Nine Personality Types.* New York: Bantam Books, 1999.

Rodgers, Richard, and Oscar Hammerstein II. "This Nearly was Mine," performed by Ezio Pinza in *South Pacific,* 1949.

Rohr, Richard. *The Naked Now: Learning to See as the Mystics See.* New York: Crossroads Publishing Company, 2009.

Rubin, Danny, and Harold Ramis. *Ground Hog Day.* DVD. Columbia Pictures, 1993.

Ruiz, Don Miguel. *The Four Agreements: A Practical Guide to Personal Freedom.* San Rafael, CA: Amber-Allen Publishing, 1997.

Sacks, Jonathan. *The Dignity of Difference: How to Avoid the Clash of Civilizations.* London, UK: Continuum, 2003.

Schleifer, Hedy and Yumi. Adventure in Intimacy Workshop. Miami, FL.

Schneider, Sarah Yehudit. *You are What You Hate: A Spiritually Productive Approach to Enemies.* Israel: A Still Small Voice, 2009.

Scott, Susan. *Fierce Conversations Achieving Success at Work & in Life, One Conversation at a Time.* Penguin Group/Viking Studio, 2002.

Seale, Alan. Founder/CEO, The Center for Transformational Presence, Topsfield, MA.

See, Lisa. *Peony in Love.* New York: Random House, 2007.

Senge, Peter, and others. *Presence: Human Purpose and the Field of the Future.* Cambridge, MA: Society for Organizational Learning, 2004.

Shange, Ntozake. *For Colored Girls Who Have Considered Suicide / When the Rainbow Is Enuf.* New York: Scribner Poetry, 1975.

Shlain, Tiffany. *Connected: Autoblogography about Love, Death & Technology.* The Moxie Institute and Impact Partners, 2011.

Shulman, Jason. *Kabbalistic Healing: A Path to an Awakened Soul.* Rochester, VT: Inner Traditions, 2004.

Siebold, Steve. *How Rich People Think.* Montgomery County, OH: London House, 2010.

Slater, Jonathan. *Mindful Jewish Living: Compassionate Practice.* New York: Aviv Press, 2007.

Solomon, Syble. *www.moneyhabitudes.com/*

Soloveitchik, Joseph B. *Lonely Man of Faith*. New York: Doubleday, 1965.

Starhawk. *Truth or Dare: Encounters with Power, Authority, and Mystery*. New York: HarperOne, 1989.

Stevens, Barry. *Don't Push the River: It Flows by Itself*. Moab, UT: Real People Press, 1970.

Sylvers, Leon, Stephen Shockley, and William Shelby. "And the Beat Goes On," performed by The Whispers. Produced by Dick Griffey, Solar, 1979.

Tillich, Paul. *Love, Power and Justice: Ontological Analyses and Ethical Applications*. New York: Oxford University Press, 1954.

Tolle, Eckhart. *The Power of Now: A Guide to Spiritual Enlightenment*. Novato, CA: New World Library, 2004.

Towne, Robert. *Personal Best*. DVD. Geffen Pictures, 1982.

Twohy, David, and Danielle Alexandra. *G.I. Jane*. Trap-Two-Zero Productions, 1997.

Wedemeyer, Richard A., and Ronald Jue. *The Inner Edge: How to Integrate Your Life, Your Work, and Your Spirituality for Greater Effectiveness and Fulfillment*. New York: McGraw-Hill, 2004.

Weil, Simone. French philosopher and Christian mystic writer, 1909-1943.

Weissman, Steven, and Rosemary Weissman. *Meditation, Compassion & Lovingkindness: An Approach to Vipassana Practice*. Samuel Weiser, 1996.

Whitney, Diana, and Amanda Trosten-Bloom. *The Power of Appreciative Inquiry: A Practical Guide to Positive Change*. San Francisco, CA: Berrett-Koehler Publishers, 2003.

Winkler, Gershon. *The Way of the Boundary Crosser: An Introduction to Jewish Flexidoxy*. Jason Aronson, 2005.

Young, William P. *The Shack*. Newbury Park, CA: Windblown Media, 2007.

Zander, Rosamund Stone, and Benjamin Zander. *The Art of Possibility: Transforming Professional and Personal Life*. Harvard Business School Press, 2000.

Zeller, David. "I Am Alive," from *Aliveness: Chants by David Zeller*, 2008.